IN PRAIS₁
iN A M₁

Not knowing much about MS I found the book a ⟍   ⟋ insight to the life of an MS sufferer but with a twist of humour. Bob was inspirational, he never let himself become the victim of his condition and he could find the funny side in some of the horrific and embarrassing situations he found himself exposed to. The message Bob is trying to conveying throughout the book is not to give up but have a positive attitude with 'dog eared perserverance'!

Emma King
Toulouse, France

A humorous and honest portrayal of one man, his family and his relationship with MS. This insightful description of life in Cheshire in the 1960s is an amusing trip down memory lane and reminds us that every family is unique in their own way. His positive approach and engaging style of writing had me smiling and laughing with every page.

Jane Noble Knight
(Author & Best seller of The Pilgrim Mother)

What a nice, charming man Bob appears to be and the light hearted way in which he is dealing with the devastating MS is very amusing and heartwarming! What a great idea to share his story in book form.

Linda McPherson
Garmouth, Moray, ScotlandMcP

"I really enjoyed the first 3 chapters of your dad's book. He certainly had a way with words! –

Sarah Westlake
Senior Editor, MS Society

"As a Well-being and Resilience Consultant I found this book rich with positive thinking and anecdotal humour. Written in a narrative style Bob takes us on a honest journey, where we discover what life was like for him, his family and community whilst living life with MS. He demonstrates, how light heartedness can transcend physical limitations and difficult times to bat of hopeless feelings and awkward moments. I was inspired by BOBs inherent resilience and the underlying message "never be defined by your condition". A delightful book that expresses the human spirit at its best, courageous and unique.

Karen Oehme,
Regional Coordinator and Book Reviewer for ISMA
(International Stress Management Association)

Acknowledgements

I have thought long and hard about this section and I would truly like to thank my dad for making me the person I am today. He may not have been around for the last 25 years but his true grit approach to things I have inherited and so I had to publish this for him as a massive thank you, for everything.

I thank my friends around me (you all know who you are) that have helped with the design of the cover and listened to my asking them questions all the time about does this look right or should I do it this way and of course for Tanya who has been a god send to me with my ever changing colours.

I want to just say thank you for everyone for reading this book and making my dads dream come true

James Roberts (Bob) Worthington
1933 - 1988

AN INSPIRATIONAL
LAUGH OUT LOUD
ACCOUNT OF HOW MS AFFECTED
ONE MAN AND HIS FAMILY

Bob Worthington

"In a MeSs" by Bob Worthington

Copyright © 2014 Cathy Gordon

freshlookmanagement@gmail.com

Editors: Sian-Elin Flint-Freel (sianelin.flintfreel@gmail.com)

Proofreader: Sian-Elin Flint-Freel (sianelin.flintfreel@gmail.com)

Cover Design and typesetting: Tanya Bäck (www.tanyabackdesigns.com)

All rights reserved. No part of this publication may be reproduced, stored in a retrieval system, or transmitted in any form or by any means, electronic, mechanical, photocopying, recording or otherwise, without the prior written permission of the copyright owner.

First published 2014 in the United Kingdom by Cathy Gordon

freshlookmanagement@gmail.com

ISBN (print): 9781783014644

ISBN (ebook): 9781783014637

Events, locales and conversations have been recreated from my father's memories. In order to maintain their anonymity in some instances I have changed the names of individuals and places, I may have changed some identifying characteristics and details such as physical properties, occupations and places of residence.

COnTeNTs

Foreword

Well, Dad, who would have thought?

This book was written by my father some 30 years ago and, sadly, he passed over 25 years ago, not getting the chance to share his sense of humour, life trials and tribulations with a wider audience.

However, I believe that now is the time to share some of his stories with you. We, as a family, may not have had the traditional life at a time when 'mum stayed at home and dad went to work' but we never needed for anything. Our home was full of love and it just turned out that really mad things happened to us. Quite rightly, Dad thought it a great idea, during his days of not being able to walk, to sit in an old, worn armchair in front of a window for many, many hours, remembering all these stories, and to put them into a book so that everyone could enjoy our story with 'MS'.

Here's to you, Dad. I needed to do this to carry on your memory, not only for our family but for all your friends and all the many others I know who loved you dearly. I also want to share these laughs with people who didn't know Dad; to hopefully give someone else out there with this 'MS' thing a chuckle whilst they are sitting in their armchairs watching the world go by and, hey, maybe inspire them to put pen to paper and share their mishaps as well.

Cathy Gordon
May 2014

Introduction

This is my story of a disease or, to be more accurate, my story of how this disease affected the lives of one man and his family. Multiple Sclerosis attacks many thousands of people in the United Kingdom alone so I believe that the majority of the general public will have at least a passing knowledge of its physical effects. I have no ambition, even should I have the detailed information and skill, to write a diatribe of symptoms, possible and impossible cures (of which there would appear to be many, though none proven) for this disease. I simply wish to tell my story of the disease from the inside as it were and, therefore, references to myelin sheaths, sensory fibres, sunflower seed oil, gluten-free diets, will be kept to an absolute minimum.

cHApTEr 1

"Your turn to fetch the coal."

This sentence was to be my unlikely introduction to the disease that would ultimately dictate not only the course that my life would follow but also that of my young wife and yet-to-be-conceived children. At the time that Sylvia, my young wife, asked me to fuel the fire I was 25 years old, the classic age for Multiple Sclerosis to give the first indication of its presence. I had met and married Sylvia some two years previously in Essex, where we had both been employed by a large company manufacturing, amongst other things, electronic equipment for the armed forces. After a short honeymoon in Bournemouth I had brought my new wife to my hometown of Walkden, about seven miles north-west of Manchester, to begin married life.

Our 'nest' was a flat above two shops which were part of a terrace of ten on the main street of the town. One of the two shops sold millinery, my mother being the milliner; the other one was a dry cleaners, where Sylvia became manageress. The flat, not very large (the shops were very small), was heated by one open fire in the living room and it was for this that Sylvia wanted me to fetch coal. I descended the flight of stairs that led from our home to a small kitchen to the rear of Mother's shop where she, during the working day, made cups of tea or complete meals, when required, for herself and my father. Dad was the proprietor of a gentlemen's outfitters (this was his advertised claim but, as in fact the property was owned by his neighbour, Barclays Bank, his claim was not strictly true) on the opposite side of the main street. This staircase was the only access to the flat and we were forced to use it on all occasions, be it entertaining family or friends or, as on this particular occasion, to carry coal from the small shed in which it was stored in the 'Coronation Street'-style backyard of the building. I collected the shovel from behind the door and went to the 'coal 'ole' in the yard. I prepared my swing, intent on gathering a good shovelful of the needed fuel. My swing started but, at the same moment, my sense of balance deserted me and, consequently, I accompanied the shovel in its flight. I recovered to find myself lying amongst the coal. On inspection, I was a little dirty but unhurt so, picking myself up, I gathered more coal, ran back up the staircase, fed the fire and amused Sylvia by telling her of my fall.

We gave no more thought to this incident and it was in no way connected, or so we believe, with the reason for the visit I made to our local doctor six or seven weeks later. I had noticed during these weeks a tingling sensation, initially in my feet and lower legs, but soon spreading to my fingers, hands and lower arms. I would not have bothered our overworked medic but it was becoming increasingly difficult to hold and manipulate many of the objects that human beings, in contrast to all the other animals on 'God's good earth', require to help them through even an average day. I had struggled with and dropped a wide range of things from a ball-point pen (without which it was impossible to write the reports that were demanded by the company that employed me as a service engineer) to my sister's first- born. No-one demanded that I held this little bundle. However, after I had dropped the baby, without injury to the baby or myself I hasten to add, there was a strong consensus of opinion that demanded that I must not come within 50 yards of my niece. The disability was also interfering with my studies at the local technical college I attended on three evenings of every week in an attempt to make good my misspent time at grammar school. So off I went to seek the professional advice of my general practitioner.

He listened to my chronicle of accidents and, without even a pretence of an examination, he said he would arrange an appointment for me as an outpatient at Salford Royal Infirmary.

A number of weeks elapsed before I was summoned to the higher league of doctors. I arrived at 'Outpatients' at my allotted time and spent the obligatory two hours waiting in the company of other patients, many of whom appeared to have difficulty in walking. 'Poor, poor souls,' I can remember thinking. I was, in due course and in the fullness of time, given a very thorough examination. This first division of doctors seemed to have a great interest in and asked many questions on what they referred to as my 'waterworks'.

"I don't know anything about the works itself", I proudly told them, "but we are very lucky in this area as every drop of our water comes from Thirlmere and it's said to be the softest water in Britain."

They then lost all interest in the waterworks, especially when I mentioned my fall in the 'coal 'ole' (or 'fuel storage bunker' as they referred to it). They insisted that I gave every detail of this accident. I was mystified at their interest in the waterworks but the answers I gave to their queries must have pleased them as the captain of the team approached me as soon as I had dressed and said,

"Thank you for answering all our questions. We have a few more tests we would like to carry out and to enable us to do these we would need you to stay in the hospital for 24 hours."

"What, now?" I gulped. "I will have to telephone my wife to see if it would be all right."

The doctor smiled. "Oh no, Mr Worthington, it will be two or three weeks before we have a vacant bed."

"Well, that should be OK then. Could you tell me what the tests will be? I mean, will they hurt? My wife is sure to ask."

"It's nothing for you or your wife to worry about," he said.

"Thank you, doctor," I came back, "but what will be tests be?"

"The lumbar puncture," he snapped.

I was none the wiser but it fell in with their interests – Water Board then National Coal Board and now the Forestry Commission!

When I received a letter requesting my attendance for the 24 hours in hospital, two months had passed and with them had gone all the tingling sensations, leaving me as steady as Gibraltar and neither baby nor ball-point dropped for weeks.

I was to learn, within a few hours of taking up residence in 'Men's Medical', that a lumbar puncture, or 'lumbar punch' as we inmates referred to it, had no connection with timber. It was a very common test (at least in my ward) which 90% of my fellow patients had had or were about to partake in its mysteries. To me, if to no-one else, 'the punch' was shrouded in mystery. It seemed to be regarded as a mixture of an initiation rite prior to the actual punch and a status symbol afterwards. I was prepared for the impending experience with stories from my fellow patients of both categories (that is, pre and post-punch) of the excruciating pain that accompanied the insertion of a needle, similar in size and construction to a garden syringe, into the spinal column and of the violent headaches that followed should you raise your head even a fraction of an inch from the pillow within 24 hours of the insertion. I went to the toilet immediately before the dreaded operation, which was carried out with the minimum of fuss as I lay on a bed in the open ward. Well, I did not raise my head from the pillow, not even a thousandth of an inch, and so I did not test the violent headache threat but, as a devout, practising coward with a negative threshold of pain, I can honestly report that the insertion of the 'garden syringe' into my spine gave me only the slightest discomfort.

Three days (or 72 hours) later, during which time my head had remained riveted to my pillow (a mistake could have been made in the time span due to the violent headaches), a doctor appeared at my bedside.

"Good afternoon, Mr Worthington, and how do we find you today?" he asked, studying the clipboard he had taken from the foot of my bed.

Overcoming the desire to give him the sort of answer he must have received on asking this question from "silly idiots" I gave him a sensible reply,

"I'm fine doctor and how are you?"

This was my standard reply to any member of the medical fraternity. It seemed to put them at their ease!

"We have completed all our tests now and have found some irregularities in the composition of your spinal column juices," he continued, ignoring my question.

"Is that bad or good?"

"Not too bad but I'm afraid it's not the type of complaint where we can go in and put things in order," he confessed.

"Don't worry," I said, very relieved that they did not want to use their knives. "I'm feeling very fit after my week in here. Do I go home?" I mention that I had been with them a week, as this was the man who had said two months previously that in two to three weeks I would be in hospital for 24 hours. He did not object so I asked no further questions nor showed any interest in my prognosis. I packed my bag and returned to the bosom of my young wife, a place I had come to love.

No name was given to my trouble but then I made no further enquiries to either my local GP or the hospital. I was asked, when leaving the hospital, to re-visit their Outpatients Department at some time in the future. I think they said three months but I did not attend. I simply put the whole episode out of my thoughts. Even with hindsight I have no regrets. I am very happy that I was, at that time as I hope I am today, the type of person who is able to ignore that sort of signal and carry on regardless. I certainly subscribed, in those Elysian days, to the school of thought that believes that death is nature's way of suggesting that we slow down. Now that I am older and wiser, my beliefs have changed only a little. If there had been a cure for my philosophy then, things would have been very different. Praise be to heaven that, like MS, no cure has been found (yet).

If I had been told that I was suffering from Multiple Sclerosis I would not have known what those unattractive words forecast. I say unattractive words but the name of my disease has a certain ring. It sounds less like a disease than the names of many present-day sports stars: I can imagine Vitus Gerilitis[1] versus Multiple Sclerosis in the men's singles final at Wimbledon. I am quite sure, however, that should I have been told from which disease I suffered, some well-meaning person would have given me chapter and verse of what would, or could happen in the future. Quite frankly, I did not want to know. Then, as now, I can wait. I am in no sort of hurry.

And so, in happy ignorance, our life carried on. I progressed in my career. I changed employers but not wives; in fact, we used most of our spare time in that pleasant pastime that makes cricket and football my second and third favourite hobbies — and I do not mean fishing!

We left the flat to buy our first house. It was a three-bedroomed, semi-detached house situated in a pleasant village on the south side of Manchester, just inside the Cheshire boundary. We were among the early 'settlers' but the population grew rapidly as did the new housing estates, without any thought for the environment, in ever-increasing numbers in the late '50s and early '60s.

It was during this period that our 'hobby' bore fruit. Sylvia presented me or, as we male chauvinists prefer, I presented Sylvia with a baby girl. When our daughter was two years old we sold the house to buy a bungalow. Whilst this move was not unwelcome, it was more or less forced upon us by economic factors. It was the old Micawber syndrome, you know, the one about earning 20 shillings[2] and spending 20 shillings and sixpence.

---

1 A Lithuanian American professional tennis player who was successful in the 70s and 80s.

2 A former monetary unit in the UK. There were 20 shillings to the pound and 12 pence in a shilling.

cHApTEr 2

We purchased a bungalow in a small town, still on the south side of Manchester in north Cheshire but a few miles deeper into the county. As I have said, the principal reason for the move was lack of money so, naturally, we bought a more expensive property! This action brought us but a few small problems. The factors that resulted in our decision to move had their roots way back in the early days of our married life.

Whilst we were living in the flat, my father had arranged a limited overdraft facility with his bank who, of course, was the landlord of his business premises. The terms of this overdraft which Dad arranged for me, the maximum value of which was £200, were that my account would be in credit within two years. As we had lived in the flat for a little more than two years and a little less than five years in our first house, Mr Edgeworth, Dad's bank manager, had some justification in being a little concerned that my account was still very much in debt.

"I shouldn't really reveal to you the exact state of the account", he said to Father one day when, during a visit to Dad's shop, he raised the subject of my finances.

"Don't worry," said Dad. "I'm sure I have only to ask Bob when next he calls in. He will tell me."

Fortunately, Dad's assessment of his son's lack of secrecy in matters financial was correct as Mr Edgeworth needed no persuasion; he proceeded to reveal the exact amount.

"£390 17s and 9d."[3]

Whether Dad was surprised or not on hearing the exact amount he never said; at least, not to me during the discussion on finances that Father convened within a few days of learning of the details of my bank account. The outcome of my meeting with my father was a decision to 'realise some capital'. This phrase I was to use on many occasions (it made me feel a little like Charlie Clore[4]). I was convinced, on studying Father's computations, that by selling our present home and taking a larger mortgage on another property (it was my personal decision to settle for a more expensive property) it was possible to eliminate my overdraft.

Sylvia found a site where bungalows were under construction. We selected one and paid a deposit of £50 by cheque. This increased the exact amount of our overdraft to £448 17s 9d but I had used my Charlie Clore phrase on Mr Edgeworth and this, coupled with Dad's continuation as my guarantor, kept the bank manager reasonably content. The modern semi we bought 5 years previously at a cost of £1,895 we sold for £3,250. The price of the new bungalow was £3,350 so, with the help of a building society, we realised some capital — but we were to find out in the not too distant future, not a lot. The existing mortgage was settled and, after paying estate agents, solicitors and all the other expenses involved with the seemingly simple task of buying and selling a home, we deposited the better part of £1,300 in the bank. I hoped that this would go some way to put a smile back onto Mr Edgeworth's face and perhaps save Dad some embarrassment. I am sure it did both — but not for long.

Our life began and continued in our new 'nest' without the worry of an overdrawn account. I was as fit as I had ever been and this period proved to be as happy as any I could remember. This happiness was somewhat 'dented' when one day it was necessary to visit the bank to collect a new cheque book. I was driving a small, green Ford 10 van that my employers provided to enable me to visit their customers' factories in order to service the many types of industrial instruments my employer manufactured. I pulled up in front of Dad's shop next to the bank, ignoring the 'No Waiting' signs that had appeared on the town's main street since I had been a resident. I gave a quick wave to Dad, whom I could see serving a customer inside his shop and at a run I went into the bank next door.

---

3 This is £360 17 shillings and 9 pence in pre-decimalisation British currency.

4 A British financier, retailer and property magnate.

Inside I found the bank to be quite busy. Three tellers, each with a small queue in front of them and under the watchful eye of Mr Edgeworth who stood at the rear of them, did their 'telling'. I joined the shortest queue and, as it grew shorter and I came closer to the bank counter, my eyes met those of the manager over the head of the young lady who was 'telling' to the people in my queue. Mr Edgeworth nodded his head to me so I nodded mine to his. The queue moved again, this time to leave me at its head, next to the counter. I told the young lady (or should it be 'telled' the young lady) that I required a new cheque book and, as she reached down below the counter to get one, my eyes met those of Mr Edgeworth again. This time I received a nod of much greater movement so, not wanting to appear at all discourteous, I returned his nod with one of my own of similar dimensions. The young lady returned to her normal upright position, gave me, in addition to a new cheque book, an envelope, saying,

"Here is an up-to-date statement of your account. It was to be posted to you today but you might as well take it as you are here. Oh yes", she added, "I believe Mr Edgeworth would like to see you."

I leaned over the counter and whispered in a conspiratorial manner, "Mr Edgeworth is standing just to the back of you and I bet he noticed the way you have saved the bank's post money – well done. For you, I'll take this envelope and, by the way," I said in a slightly louder voice as I strained from the counter, "Mr Edgeworth has nodded his greetings to me."

As I collected my papers and moved away from the counter, I once more looked towards the bank manager but this time I managed to get my nod in first. Mr Edgeworth gave me a smile and then he moved down the bank on his side of the counter as I moved down the bank on my side. Our movement down parallel paths, separated by a couple of yards and the bank counter, continued until Mr Edgeworth's path led him into his office.

Like most bank managers' offices, Mr Edgeworth's had two entrances — one on the working side of the premises for the staff and the second one leading from the main body of the building for us lesser mortals. As Mr Edgeworth disappeared into his office, I carried on past the second door and out through the imposing front door of the bank which stood open. Back into the main street, a few rapid steps across the pavement and, with only the briefest wave to Dad still serving customers, I was in the green van, racing away. I wondered if I should have popped my head round Mr Edgeworth's door to wish him 'good day' but, as we had spent the last five minutes nodding our heads to one another like two balloons in a breeze and my van had been badly parked, I thought it unnecessary.

Much later in the day, I had the opportunity to open the envelope I had collected from the bank. I found enclosed the up-to-date statement of my account and the real reason for Mr Edgeworth's nodding head was there for the reading. Clearly laid out in columns headed pounds, shillings and pence was printed 140 in the first column, 16 in the second and 10 in the third – oh yes, and they were all printed in a nice bright shade of red! I contemplated many times but never discovered how long my bank manager sat in his office, awaiting my entrance through the customers' door.

A few days later I received a polite letter from Mr Edgeworth, requesting the pleasure of my company. He had obviously by-passed my father this time or, more likely, he had approached my parent who had advised him to 'pull me in' and lay down the gospel according to St Sterling. I attended as requested and received a lecture on the theory of banking which, in a nutshell, makes great issue of how the bankers prefer to look after our money rather than the system of which I was a practising advocate.

Once more, I had to 'realise some capital'. As we had only been in our new home a matter of months, moving house did not seem to be the number one choice this time. During the first few weeks of married life I had taken out an endowment policy for a 'rainy day' and, as we had just entered the 'monsoon season', I redeemed the policy. When reading of this episode, I may appear to be totally irresponsible with money. I submit that this is not true because I put £400 of what I received from the insurance company into the bank. This more than cleared the overdraft so, with the surplus, I took my wife and young daughter on what was to be a beautiful holiday. We spent two weeks in Blanes on the Costa Brava and spent all but a few pounds of the endowment. If this is irresponsible, then tell me what money is made for.

We arrived home from Spain very brown and very, very happy. Sylvia came home pregnant and I came home with a tingling sensation in my hands and feet.

cHApTEr 3

Over the following months, the family was increased by one; Jane Catherine now had a brother, James Leslie, and I learned to live with the 'tingles'. They came and went, if not from day to day then from week to week and, though they were there more than not, I still did not think it was anything to be concerned about. I believed that one fine day they would go, never to return. However, I began to notice other, what I now know to be symptoms, appearing. I found, for instance, that I no longer walked in straight lines. If I had not noticed, my friends and colleagues had. When walking at my side they would complain in the nicest possible way – "For God's sake, stop bumping into me!" or similar comment.

Another thing I noticed, perhaps most of all (in fact, definitely most of all) was my 'waterworks'. I realised that the doctors all those years ago in Salford did know the right questions after all. At this time, my control was not bad, at least not when compared with the almost total lack of control of later years. Let it suffice to say that I had very little warning of nature's calls. I had no 'accidents of the third kind' (which is another term, similar to 'waterworks', used in polite circles when discussing matters that concern bladders and bowels) but once or twice came perilously near.

I had a mental list of public toilets in all parts of England, Scotland and Wales as my working area covered very large parts of these countries since being made redundant by the company that had provided the little, green Ford 10 vans. Now I was employed by a company that provided a larger vehicle in the form of a Morris Oxford saloon car and I had to travel a wider area. This list of toilet locations was invaluable to my peace of mind and, undoubtedly, to the amount of soiled underclothes in Sylvia's weekly wash. If the list of public toilets failed to meet a particularly desperate call, I could, and many times did, resort to private public toilets. Many is the garage forecourt onto which I have driven at high speed, braked to a tyre-screaming halt, leapt out of the car almost before it ceased moving and shouted over my shoulder to the attendant as I ran,

"One gallon, please, and where are your toilets?" hoping and praying that I was moving in the right direction and that I would not hear, as I did many times, the shouted reply,

"It's over there but you can't use it. It's for staff only."

The first time I heard this I froze solid and so must the contents of my bladder as the desperate 'urge' disappeared instantly. I stopped in mid-flight, walked purposefully back to the car, gave the attendant my most pleasant smile and said,

"In that case, get your bloody staff to buy your bloody petrol!" and drove off in the same manner I had arrived; not in an effort to show my displeasure but in an effort to reach the next garage as my bladder was rapidly unfreezing. Yes, I kid you not. I came very, very close to an 'accident' on many, many occasions.

I never have and I am sure I never will accept this, what surely must be the most unsociable side of any disease or, to be more explicit, I am not content to be incontinent. I want to have complete control of the time when and the places where I leave my faeces — and I certainly do not want to pass water where and when 'I did not oughta'.

These accounts of near mishaps sound very light-hearted but, believe me, although I have managed to cope with most of the problems that MS has thrown up so far, perhaps not easily but with a lot of help from my family and friends, incontinence is something very different.

To illustrate my feelings, let me relate the details of an experience I had about this time that could have had all kinds of embarrassing consequences. I was, as previously stated, travelling the country by car at this time, endeavouring to sell electronic instruments to all types of industrial and educational establishments. On one evening, I left London around seven o'clock in the evening and took the

M1 motorway heading north, homeward bound. I believe in motorways. They get you to journey's end quickly. If the speedo reads 70 mph, then in one hour you have travelled (well these days, under favourable conditions) as many as eight miles! However, in those earlier days of motorways, 70 mph on the clock meant 70 miles travelled in one hour, albeit between nowhere and nowhere – I mean those rather less than popular places that the early motorways invariably linked. High-speed roads are undeniably ideal for many thousands of motorists but they are a nightmare to the sensitive incontinent — and worse to the inexperienced, unprepared, very sensitive incontinent. I must have been 15 miles from the nearest service area, with no slip roads in those miles, when I became very aware that I was in need of a place 'to go'. I proceeded that evening at a speed that, should I have maintained it for the hour should the motorway have led there, I would have been in Scotland 'afore ye'. So, a very short time later, I zoomed onto the Toddington Service Station without either a traffic or the other type of accident.

I parked the car and moved with all the speed I could muster across the car park, towards the toilets. With a quick glance at the 'Men' notice, I dashed inside and then into the first 'trap' opposite the entrance. I slammed the door of the 'trap' shut, rapidly made the necessary adjustments to my dress, sat down and enjoyed one of nature's pleasures. I relaxed, recovering from the hair-raising drive up the motorway and savouring the relief when I heard a strange but familiar sound. It only took a second before my unwilling mind was forced to accept it for what it was – the unmistakable sound; the clip-clop of high-heeled shoes just the other side of the door of this small cubicle that, in an instant, had changed from a haven to what felt like a very small prison cell. I couldn't be in the ladies' toilets! I remembered seeing 'Men' on the sign outside — but then, did I? I quickly lifted my feet from the floor; the door and walls of my 'cell' stopped at least 12 inches from the tiled floor. I sat, hugging my knees and listening to various other definitely female sounds that seemed to grow louder and closer by the second. What the hell could I do? I must choose my actions very carefully. Perhaps the best idea was to take the bull by the horns and shout – but what?

"Ladies stop! I'm a man and I've made a terrible mistake!"

But, as I had been in the place an absolute minimum of five minutes by this time, who would believe me? I could see the reports in the Sunday newspapers, hear my so-called friends saying, "Who would have thought it of Bob Worthington? I always knew he had a dark side."

It would obviously lead to divorce. How would my children manage without a Dad? I knew I would never get custody of them. I sat there for a further few minutes. I thought of all the strange happenings I had heard of in motorway service areas.

No, for the sake of my children I must not make my presence known. I then did what could have been my downfall in more ways than one. I wedged my feet between the walls of the narrow cubicle and, with a movement that the best contortionist would have found difficult, I lowered my head and shoulders between my knees and looked under the wall. Should I have lost my balance, or worse, if I had looked into the eyes of any woman who happened to look down at that moment, I expect my epitaph would have read 'He was found dead, his trousers round his ankles, his legs wrapped round his neck, in the ladies' toilet at the Toddington Service Station on the M1 Motorway: in this position a heart attack was to be expected.'

In reality, all I did see from my uncomfortable position was an even number of female shoes and lower legs, the bodies of which, from their position in relation to my assumed knowledge of the premises, were all in a sitting position. Now was my chance of escape. I lowered my feet to the floor, readjusted my clothes at speed, opened the door and stepped smartly out into the ladies toilets. If I had been able to, I would have sprinted away but, due to my slight disability, I was only able to travel at a fast stagger. I glanced down the length of the space, along the closed doors of the 'traps'. At the very instant of my glance, the furthermost door opened and out stepped a smartly dressed, middle-aged woman. Our eyes met. It was one of those rare moments when, as the saying goes, 'time stood still'. It seemed like a lifetime that our eyes held each other's gaze. Not a word passed between us, until my whirring brain suggested to me that she was as surprised to see me as I was shattered to see her. So, as if there was nothing in the least unusual in the place of our meeting, I nodded my head politely, said, "Good evening," and, walking as straight as possible, I held my head erect and staggered out of the door. Without even the briefest pause, I continued back across the car park towards my car without hearing the screams and shouts of "Stop – sex maniac!" that I was expecting. I reached the safety of the car and, within seconds, I was once more endeavouring to break the land speed record on Britain's No. 1 motorway.

Very many weeks passed before I dared to venture into this Service Station again and, even then, I ensured that I wore completely different clothing – right down to socks and underpants. I was surprised to find there was not a full police check still in operation. I had been studying all the national press and watching the television newscasts, expecting to see or hear reports of the 'Phantom of the Motorways' Ladies' Toilets'. Remember, these were the days before streakers and the permissive society. I casually inspected the toilets from the outside this time and soon discovered the reason for my near downfall. The signs were not the usual 'Ladies' and 'Gentlemen' but 'Women' and 'Men' and, from the direction I had approached them in such a hurry on that fateful evening, I had looked at the sign at the instant when it was only possible to see the last three letters of the 'Women' notice. That's my story and I have no option but to stick to it. It may not sound very convincing to you now but to me, on the evening when I was trapped inside, it would have sounded like the original 'likely story'.

The only lasting lesson I have learned from my experience at Toddington is not to think 'nudge, nudge, wink, wink,' on hearing or reading of similar happenings to other unfortunates.

cHApTEr 4

My unsteady walk became worse, as did the tingling sensation in my hands and feet. I also noticed that, on bending my head forward, a feeling not unlike a slight electric shock ran through the whole of my body. These sensations, whilst not pleasant, could by no stretch of the imagination be described as painful. Not only was I unsteady when moving, on some occasions I would wobble quite noticeably when standing supposedly quite still. I began to carry and use a walking stick, not only for the help I gained from its steadying influence when I walked, but mainly to prevent the public at large from smiling at my rolling gait and thinking, or worse saying, "Take a look at him, he's just drunk a good meal!"

The time had arrived for another visit to the medical fraternity. It was, of course, to be a different doctor from the one I had visited those 10 years ago. I attended at a new surgery in a new town and found a new system in operation. No longer did you just enter, take a seat in the doctor's waiting room and memorise the patients already present when you entered to ensure that you received your 'turn' with the doctor. This memory test was very simple during the healthy summer months but during a cold, wet winter spell at which time the world's flu and similar viruses migrate to our shores and consequently the doctors' surgeries had standing room only, it was less easy. The system I now found in operation required the prospective patient on arrival to present himself at a small 'hatch' where a receptionist would take all his particulars and in return give a small disc on which a number was stamped and only then would he take a seat, endeavouring to guess who had the disc with the number just one digit less than his and so ensure his rightful turn with the doctor. There's progress! The year of this visit of mine was the year man took a small step onto the surface of the moon.

The operation of the new system and the primary task of ensuring that your turn with the doctor was not missed when your number came up were not helped by having three different doctors drawing and treating patients from the one pool of numbered patients. Each doctor had a private office and outside each was an illuminated sign that announced when the next patient was required for consultation. As I waited, I found that the numbered discs were very soon redundant as certain people in the middle of a course of treatment had to have audience with one particular 'quack' (sorry, doctor). In any case, there was a Mrs Jones, of elephantine proportions, saying,

"I will only see Dr Smith – that new Dr Singh is too young to treat me! I'm not taking my clothes off in front of him!"

On this afternoon, I was informed by a charming lady (not Mrs Jones) that there were only two numbers less than mine so I gave all my attention to the proceedings. An old gentleman came out from my chosen doctor's office, the sign lit up and an elderly lady entered to take his place. In only a couple of seconds, the sign illuminated again. No-one appeared aware that the elderly lady failed to reappear before a younger woman, accompanied by two small children, arose from her seat and Mummy ushered her offspring through the doorway into the doctor's consulting room. I was puzzled by the apparent disappearance of the first older woman and passed the next 10 minutes trying to work out the layout of the building. There were no windows through which I could check for other doors but then I was almost sure that the rear wall of the office formed part of the rear external wall of the whole structure of the building, which in turn formed part of the boundary of our local sports ground — unlikely to be any doors there.

I was about to enlist the aid of my fellow patients when the sign illuminated.

"It's your turn now" said one of the helpful ladies.

I hesitated, waiting for the young family to emerge but they did not. The door stayed ominously closed.

"Come on luv, we can't wait all day," said a Mrs Jones, giving my shoulder a gentle prod.

I stood up and took a couple of slow, unsteady steps towards the door of the office in which people entered only to disappear. I stopped, turned to face the waiting patients and said,

"I don't know if any of you have noticed but no-one has come out of there recently. Now I'm willing to go in to investigate but if I'm not out in five minutes, call the police".

Embarrassed by my show of bravery, I turned, opened the door and advanced through it. I quickly inspected the room, which was empty except for the doctor sitting at a large desk, deeply engrossed in a large, fat file. Without looking up, but indicating two chairs on my side of the desk, he said,

"Shut the door, Mr Worthington. Have a seat. I'll be with you in a moment."

He continued to study the file whilst I tried to look under his desk for the missing patients. The doctor looked up.

"Well, Mr Worthington, how are you?"

Half the time I had allowed before the constabulary would be summoned had passed. Smiling, I leaned forward over his desk, straining to see if he had the bodies hidden between his feet. Should I challenge him outright? No, I would play it cool.

"Oh, I'm fine doctor. How are you?"

"Now relax, Mr Worthington. What has brought you to see me?"

I sat back in the chair. "What time is it?" I asked.

The puzzled look that came to the doctor's face brought me back to the doctor's question.

"I've got a tingling sensation in my hands and feet, I'm very unsteady on my legs and I lose my balance very often," I gabbled out without a pause for breath.

He studied the file again for a moment and then asked, "Is it the same as before or would you say worse?"

"Yes," I said. Then realising that my answer was no answer, at least not a sensible one, I mentioned, "It's got much worse these last few months."

"It says here you were an inpatient at Salford Royal Infirmary," he said, touching the file. "I think, perhaps, I'd better make arrangements for you to pay them another visit."

Good, at least he was not looking on me as his next victim. Yes, five in one afternoon would be too much.

"Whatever you think," I said as I rose from the chair.

"But perhaps I'd better check your reflexes. Just come through here."

He stood up and took a couple of steps away from the desk. In spite of my unsteadiness, I spun round and reached for the door and escape. As was to be expected, I fell, apex over appendix, and landed with a crash against the door. The wooden chair went in the opposite direction, making an even louder crash as it came to rest against the doctor's desk. The doctor rushed over to deliver what I thought was going to be the fatal blow.

"Be careful!" he cried.

"Don't you worry, I can take care of myself."

I was about to make a grab for his legs but, in the nick of time, I noticed that, as I had been doing my pirouette, he had opened a white door in one of the room's white walls. With not a little difficulty and with a joint effort, the chair was uprighted and I was safely seated on it.

"Are you sure you've not hurt yourself?" the doctor enquired before he turned his attention to the two women and two children who had emerged from the open door of his inner examination room. He directed his next remarks to them, "Have that prescription made up and take all of the tablets. The trouble should have cleared up within a few days but if it hasn't come in to see me again."

So that was the explanation. They had been in a room within a room, I realised. The re-materialised patients left us and the doctor helped me through the white door and carried out the tests on my reflexes. I then took my leave. As I walked through the waiting room I was very pleased not to find it full of blue uniforms. I had been with the doctor over 20 minutes and my crash against the door, I felt, would have sent someone running to dial 999.

The doctor was as good as his word and a couple of weeks later I revisited the Outpatients Department at Salford Infirmary. This time the obligatory two hours' wait had been abolished. It had been replaced by an obligatory three hours' wait. After completing this entrance test, I was asked the same old questions by a young doctor and then informed that, as the specialist was not in the hospital, I would need to make a further appointment in order to see him.

I do not believe there should be a need for private medicine but the thought of more of the 'obligatories' made me throw my principles to the wind and make a private appointment to see the specialist. Within days, I arrived in Manchester's equivalent to Harley Street and, within minutes, I was in the consulting rooms of one of the north of England's leading neurologists. I received the full red carpet treatment. The only thing omitted was the details of the disease that was attacking my central nervous system. I made three more visits to this very kind gentleman doctor, with whom I have no complaint, before I was to learn the nature of my disease. At the end of his examination, he prescribed the only treatment I have received under the National Health Service specifically for MS. It was a drug called 'Synactin Depot', a cortisone derivative, and I was to have two injections every week. Over the next four years, these 'jabs' were administered by a number of nurses at a variety of hospitals dotted over the large area I visited during my working travels until, later, my wife Sylvia learned the 'art'. Meanwhile, I carried small quantities of this drug with me at all times so that if I was due for the treatment I would call in at a convenient hospital, present my credentials and the drug at 'Outpatients' and usually, with little trouble, a nurse would be provided to carry out the injection.

This was even carried out behind the 'Iron Curtain' when I visited Czechoslovakia to work on my employers' stand at an international trade fair. The medical staff at the exhibition ground were very kind and helpful and asked many questions about my trouble but, as I knew nothing, I could tell them very little. In retrospect, I guess they knew only too well what my trouble was but, as it was obvious that I did not, they were not prepared to tell me the nature of my illness which my English doctors had withheld.

It was this 'treatment' that, four years later I am reliably informed, led to a grave shortage of calcium in my bones that led to a compression fracture of my lumbar vertebrae that led to a visit to the osteopath, which led to a few days in Crewe Hospital with its enemas. Eat your heart out James Burke[5]!

---

5 A British broadcaster, science historian, author and television producer who is known for, amongst other things, his documentary television series 'Connections'.

cHApTEr 5

Two or three years passed with the tingles sometimes worse and sometimes not too bad but I was completely ignorant of my disease. Another flaw in my degenerating bodily systems appeared: my vision became a little blurred. This was most apparent when driving. It would be necessary when wishing to join a major road, such as a motorway from a slip road, to look back over my right shoulder and this was the time when not only would I see 'blurred', I would see 'double'. I was aware of the inherent danger in this malfunction of my eyes and took even greater care to ensure that all of the six carriageways carrying vehicles in my direction (on the 12-lane motorway) viewed over my right shoulder were absolutely traffic-free — or that at most no more than two identical cars were in the two outside lanes!

I sheepishly attended the surgery to get the medical reason for my faulty vision. The doctor gave my eyes a good 'going over' and began his explanation with the words, "As we approach 40." I took no further notice of his subsequent theories. If he could not see from just one glance that I was a mere boy, barely 35 years old – approaching 40 indeed! – "The man was a fool," I thought. So again, I did not pursue an answer to my difficulties with the people who doubtless knew what was at the bottom of my health problem.

It came to pass that Sylvia was the first to be given 'the word' by the medics. During a visit by Sylvia to our GP on a totally different matter, in which he dealt with her (or was it really my), request for the 'pill', the doctor mentioned the subject of my health.

"The type of Multiple Sclerosis that your husband has . . . ."

Sylvia did not hear or could not remember the remainder of his prognosis; she was shattered. She knew the effects of this disease. In the company where she had last been employed, a colleague had MS diagnosed and in 18 months had deteriorated from quite an active man to a wheelchair invalid. Sylvia joined me in the car where I waited whilst she had consulted with the doctor. The shock she had received on hearing his words gave me not even the slightest tremor. In as calm a manner as she could manage she endeavoured to convey to me what the disease Multiple Sclerosis was all about.

It is very true that there are none so deaf as those that do not want to hear, especially those whose spouses explain to them that they are the victims of a crippling disease of which they have never heard. Now, should the doctor have said, "The type of cholera or bubonic plague," or even if he had said she was too late with the pill (as in 'I am 3 months with child'), I would perhaps have reacted in a similar manner as Sylvia had. But for Multiple Sclerosis – nothing!

It was not until later in the day, when I referred to the Readers' Digest Great Encyclopaedic Dictionary, that I began to admit that there may be a slight chance that the 'tingles' and those annoying symptoms had a message for me.

A few days later, on my way home from a successful visit to South Birmingham Polytechnic, I telephoned Sylvia to ask her to make an immediate appointment to see the neurologist I had been visiting privately in Manchester. This sudden request was brought about because, although the visit to Birmingham had been successful business-wise (I had gained the promise of an order), this was in spite of the fact that I had staggered, trembled, spilt cups of tea over most of the college and its staff and, as a finale, had all but urinated in the Head of Mechanical Engineering's office. In fairness to Sylvia, I must add that she had been pressing me to take this action since our GP had so casually let the 'cat out of the bag'. Two days later (remember I was a private patient) I was with the specialist and he confirmed that indeed Multiple Sclerosis had been diagnosed more than 10 years previously during my first visit to Salford Royal Infirmary. Let me say at this point that I totally agree with the doctors' decisions not to tell me of their findings until it was forced upon them. I feel sure that I would have denied myself some of the nicer things in life, not the least of these being two children. To be frank though, I wished that during this visit he had taken me off Synactin Depot as this, whilst reducing the length of my story by a couple of chapters, would, I believe, have saved me from the only real pain I have suffered (if not directly) from MS. A ha'porth[6] of prevention is better than a ton of cure.

Now that we knew what our troubles were or, more importantly, what our future more or less would bring, I made a flying visit to Glasgow to tell my Managing Director of the diagnosis, the symptoms of which, along with the rest of the company's employees, he had in polite and caring silence observed, gradually watching me grow more and more disabled. As the fellow from Stratford had said (or nearly said) "If you have tears to shed, then shed them now". My news was received with sympathy and, if nothing else, prepared the way for the tendering of my resignation some months later.

It was on the return flight I discovered (at least at the time I believed I had discovered) a cure for cowardice. Thirty minutes into the one-hour flight and at about 15,000 feet, the Captain's voice came over the intercom,

"There is heavy weather ahead and Manchester Airport is likely to be closed."

At the same time, the 'Fasten Your Safety Belts Please' light illuminated. Only two short weeks ago I would have forced my way onto and done my utmost to take full control of the flight deck. I had not spent three years in Her Majesty's Royal Airforce, albeit as a ground radar mechanic, for nothing! Fortunately for passengers and crew, I did not give a monkey's! I am not proud to admit it but that evening, if they had opened the door there and then, I would have been very willing to walk home – "Mind the first step, Bob. It's a big 'un."

I made no secret of my new-found knowledge, except to my immediate family. My father had died from the big 'C' before my symptoms had begun to appear and, whilst I was in reasonably frequent contact with my mother and my only sister Glenys, when my obvious difficulties in walking and my once nasty habit of dropping nieces (of which by this time I had two) were discussed in general, never were they discussed in particular, at least not in my presence. The full details, however, could not be withheld for long.

The opportunity to give them the information arose a few weeks later, quite easily, during another talk with Mum, the subject to which it was very much connected. After many long hours of discussion, Sylvia and I decided we should buy a shop. This was a natural choice, and probably inevitable, because I belonged to a family who came from generations of shopkeepers. Not only did we belong to a nation of shopkeepers but also a family of shopkeepers.

---

6 An amount that can be bought with half a penny.

We began to search the newspapers' 'Business for Sale' columns. We found many shops of all descriptions, all with excellent prospects. We also found, as we should have expected, that we were short of the necessary finance and, after my earlier experiences with banks and their managers, I felt sure that any request I made in this direction would be met with cries of "You have got to be joking". When my father had died, Mum had been forced to (Now, what was that term? – got it!) "realise all her capital" and I hoped she would loan me a piece of the family fortune which, when added to the money we would raise from the sale of our bungalow, would prove enough to buy a thriving business. The chance to put the proposition to Mum came the following Saturday.

Sylvia and I were taking Mum on a visit to her daughter, a journey of 20 or so miles. I was driving with Mum at my side and Sylvia and our two children in the back.

"Mum," I said when half of the miles were behind us, "we are thinking of buying a shop."

If she was surprised by my statement she gave no outward indication. Perhaps she had expected us to think along these lines, after all, she and Dad had also been shopkeepers.

"What type of shop have you been thinking of?" she asked.

"Well, something in the food line we thought, so that Sylvia can manage it on her own." Mum was silent, so I went on, "It's just in case my health gets worse."

I still avoided mentioning the fact that I knew what my disease had been diagnosed as. I was sure Mum would have full knowledge of Multiple Sclerosis and I was worried about giving her the news that her 'little boy' had become one of its victims.

"We've been to look at a couple of grocers but they want a hell of a lot of money for them," I continued, mainly to fill the silence.

I believe that Mother was not altogether sure (I can now understand why) that we were aware of all the pitfalls encountered when running even the smallest business as she and Dad had sheltered their children from the ever-present problems of shopkeeping. Eventually she spoke, "The trouble with food shops these days is that, if you are not very careful, the multiples will drive you out of business."

There was a choking noise from the rear seat of the car from where Sylvia had been silently following our conversation but Mum's last observation could not pass unchallenged.

"But it's the multiples that are driving us into business," she choked.

I was surprised but pleased at Sylvia's first words since I had broached the subject of our future plans. (Some eight or nine years later, when I first thought of writing this story, its title was to be 'How the Multiples Drove us into Business' – derived from this remark of Sylvia's). Sylvia and I laughed nervously. Mum was naturally mystified by our sudden amusement.

"What's funny?" she asked sharply.

The moment I had looked for yet dreaded had arrived.

"What Sylvia is trying to tell you is that I've got Multiple Sclerosis."

"Who told you that?" Mum's question sounded silly then, as no doubt it does now. She was upset, as her next question when I answered her last one proved.

"The doctor," I replied.

"Are you sure?" she almost shouted.

"Yes, Mum, I'm sure," Perhaps not very kindly adding, "It's not the sort of thing you get wrong."

The question of buying businesses paled into insignificance as my disease was discussed in all its aspects. Mum had known a young chap who had MS and she could not be stopped from telling us his medical life story.

We arrived at my sister's home but the inquisition continued. I began to feel as if I had let the family down somehow by contracting this dreadful disease. I am absolutely sure that Mother and sister had no intention of giving this impression. They were just as concerned as Sylvia and I were on first hearing the unpleasant facts. They wanted to know if I had informed my employer so I gave them the details of my flight to Glasgow (omitting to tell them of my short-lived desire to alight from the aeroplane at 15,000 feet above the Lake District) and of my boss's understanding. Mum was very relieved that I had not received 'the sack'. Right up to the time when my pride, more than my employer's desire, forced me to hand in my resignation, she wanted me to stay in a position that would present me with a cheque at the end of each month. Just like a mother!

Our decision to buy a shop was not mentioned once during that day but, during the following weeks, Sylvia and I spent all our spare time scouring the adverts and visiting shops that, for various reasons, were on the market.

On a later visit to my sister's, Glenys suddenly said, "Mum tells me you are thinking of buying a business."

It came as manna from heaven. At least the family had discussed our ambitions in our absence and not laughed them 'out of court'. My sister and brother-in-law were already in business. Glenys's husband was a motor mechanic and, a few years earlier, they had bought a small garage with a little financial assistance from our parents and, since then, with a great deal of hard work and sacrifice, they had built it up into quite a prosperous venture. It was possibly their experience that helped them to lend their support to our plans.

"We," she said, speaking for herself and her husband, "have talked it over and think it's a good idea. We've made a few enquiries and feel that your best bet is to try to get a sub-post office. At least you would then know that there would always be a salary at the end of the month."

"And that alone should please Mum," I said.

Our spirits soared. Not only was member of the family on our side, she was offering helpful and constructive advice.

cHApTEr 6

From this time, we concentrated all our energies in the search for sub-post offices, regardless of the type of business to which they were attached; if they were for sale then we were interested. We became friendly with our area sub-postmaster. This was not difficult, as he was a regular at our 'local' where I very occasionally, certainly no more than once a day, would call for a 'swift half' and Sylvia was a regular visitor to his shop, collecting the family allowance, paying our newspaper bills and such.

Our friendly neighbourhood sub-postmaster and his wife gave us lots of invaluable information; they introduced us to the complex mysteries involved with the running of a sub-post-office with its Friday evening balance, during which weekly event every stamp, postal order, insurance stamp (still in use during our first years), premium savings bonds, and all the other seemingly hundreds of different items held in stock at even the humblest of post offices, have to be counted. The resulting figures are then used in the computing of the 'Balance' along with other figures such as pensions paid, savings bank deposits and withdrawals and so on and so on, and then, lastly, the cash in hand. According to Post Office regulations, all these figures, when entered into the correct lines, in the correct columns, on the correct page in the large cash book provided should balance to the penny — need I say, they never did! Oh yes, my sister was correct. We would have a salary cheque arrive every month-end but, what with the extra grey hairs, loss of sleep on Friday nights and glorious shouting matches (during which I was to learn the full breadth of Sylvia's vocabulary), it was to be a few years before our Friday evenings cooled down sufficiently to bid each other 'Goodnight' without adding a quiet, but quite audible, noun and adjective.

Enough of the day-to-day or week-to-week troubles of the operation of a sub-post office and back to our search for such a business. I cannot honestly remember a particular occasion on which an arrangement was made with Mum to borrow "X" number of pounds but we arrived at the figure which we could afford. Whether it was planned or we were just lucky, the asking price of a number of properties with our chosen type of business was within our financial reach. We found first one, visited it alone, once again with Mother and then again with our 'tame' sub-postmaster and repeated these visits to a second and then another and then another until our postmaster was much less friendly and we were beginning to feel that we were never to find 'the' one.

At last, after many weeks, we discovered the sub-post office which we were sure was the one for us. It had a few drawbacks. It was described as 'semi-rural' and it doubtless was semi-rural. In fact, by standing in the centre of the road and looking towards the shop and attractive hostelry next door, one viewed the cultivated fields behind and looked beyond to the Manchester Ship Canal, where some two or three miles away it lazily made its way through the Cheshire countryside after being freed from the industrial areas of Manchester's Trafford Park in one direction and Merseyside's Ellesmere Port in the other. It was not wise to stand contemplating this rural side of the environment too long as, on slowly turning around there spread before you one the largest chemical manufacturing complexes, certainly in Greater Manchester and possibly in the north west of England. This less pleasant view did not deter us in the least; the living accommodation was to the rear of the property. So we made our usual two further visits. Mum was not over-impressed with the property's position and was concerned about pollution of the air but, as our Post Office advisor had no strong arguments against the 'turnover' of that side of the business for which he was there to advise (by this time he would have given his full support to our purchase of a sub-post office situated on a deserted iceberg, with a private business fully stocked with sunglasses and Nivea cream), she did not completely veto the project.

The Business Transfer Agent dealing with the sale of this business had offices in a large Victorian building in the centre of Manchester and Sylvia and I made a number of visits there. As our interests progressed, we were passed from these offices to those of a solicitor and then to more offices that housed a Finance Agent (we had wished to borrow a further couple of thousand pounds for the purchase of stock etc.). I walked very unsteadily during this period but, believed, not too obviously as I felt that the men of business in a large city such as Manchester would want no dealings with a near 'cripple'. My wife was of great assistance in my hopeful deceptions; she walked slowly at all times and insisted on holding my arm whenever we moved along the many passages that honeycombed this type of building. We soon learned to manage the passages themselves but came to grief on the inevitable three or four-step staircases that littered our path along the passages. We began to feel like real members of the world of high finance and, when my sister and her husband Les found the business that we were eventually to purchase, dealt with by other estate agents and solicitors, we found we were practising even more deceits as we wished to keep both options open.

We began to receive telephone calls and visits from different 'professional' people as well as the vendors of both projects as soon as we had shown a real interest in Glenys and Leslie's choice. The calls came at all times of day and evening, some expected but the majority totally unexpected. We kept 'face' with both groups until the fateful day when we 'blew it'. I was in my small office at home, completing some paperwork for my long-suffering employer. I had instructed Sylvia before commencing my allotted task.

"Today I'm going to try to catch up on some reports that are long overdue. I am going to put all thoughts of shops and post offices out of my mind. If anyone wants me, tell them I've gone to — oh, think of somewhere — anywhere — as long as I don't have to speak to them and tell any more lies."

Sylvia went to the kitchen to wash some clothes — or to do one of the many tasks (if they are to be believed) which housewives find to do. On the wall in the kitchen was an extension of the telephone which stood at my side on my desk. It was my intention to allow Sylvia to intercept all incoming calls. I was making good progress into the large amount of paperwork that required my attention when, about mid-morning, the telephone rang.

Forgetting my carefully laid plans, on the second or third ring I picked up the receiver and, after giving the number said, "Hello, Bob Worthington speaking."

The caller had just time to give his name. It was the estate agent from the group who were dealing with the first business in which we were showing an interest.

Then my dear wife picked up her extension and also gave our telephone number and went on, "Hello, Sylvia Worthington here."

The man on the other end must have realised what had happened, as he said, "Good morning, Mrs Worthington. It was your husband I wished to speak to."

Before I had chance to make my presence on the telephone known to Sylvia, she carried out my instructions.

"Oh, I'm sorry but you can't. He's gone to London."

I very quickly put my hand over the mouthpiece and shouted through the house to her, "I'm speaking to him from here."

Sylvia's woman's logic came to her aid. I just got the telephone back to my ear when Sylvia spoke with an innocence which Sarah Bernhart could not have bettered.

"Oh . . . well . . . er . . . he's not gone. But . . . he is going!"

She then replaced her receiver and raced through the house to her shattered husband's side so as not to miss a single second of his embarrassment. Never before or since have I believed more than I did at that particular moment in that well-worn saying that has as its rhyming couplet 'weave' and 'deceive'. There were no harsh words during the conversation I then had with this estate agent but, perhaps unnecessarily, I came 'clean' and admitted that we were in negotiations for the purchase of a different property from that with which he was dealing. We politely said goodbye and he graciously wished me good luck in our new venture. All the stops were then pulled out and, using our newly learned skills, we set our undivided attention on the acquisition of the post office and village stores in the village of Hassall Green in the county of Cheshire.

We took Mum to see the property on the following Sunday afternoon. The weather that day of decision was glorious and Mum, Glenys and Les, who accompanied us on the visit, saw what was to become our future home and life at its very best.

The property which we were officially shown was in excess of 150 years old — at least the original building was but various bits and pieces had been added over the years and, though not giving the overall building a pretty appearance, it was far from ugly; the additions made it very interesting. According to the descriptive leaflets that had been printed to assist its sale, it stood in a garden of a third of an acre and this included a small tarmacadamed area to the front and side of the part of the property where the shop was situated; this was used as a car park. The width of the front garden and car park was 35 to 40 foot and this garden was 18 inches or so lower than the car park. The driveway immediately in front of the house.

Sarah Bernhardt was a French stage and early film actress, and was referred to as "the most famous actress the world has ever known."

The main thoroughfare of the village formed the boundary of the land and the shop and the house faced this road. The telephone box inevitably found in close vicinity to all post offices was, in this case, on the corner of the car park, close to the road. The accommodation (apart from the shop) afforded 4 bedrooms, stock rooms, a lounge, kitchen and (what we had learned were known as) offices. At the rear of the car park, at the side of the main building was a two-storey building that we discovered had been used over the years as a bakery and, at a different time, had been used for the rearing and keeping of pigs. Recently, it had been fitted with 'up and over' doors and was used as a garage for the present owner's family car, although it was quite long enough to hold two average-length vehicles. The second floor was just a glorified junk store. Leaning to the side of this utility brick building, on the side furthest from the main house and shop building, was a timber and asbestos garage, not in use and standing empty.

Along the full length of the property, on the same side as the utility building, was the feature that was to bring business as well as pleasure in different ways to all members of the family. I refer to the Trent and Mersey Canal. It also was in excess of 150 years old. The property I am endeavouring to describe was, I imagine, first planned and erected very soon after an engineer named Telford planned and supervised the digging of the canal. His plan would have shown a double lock at this location but, 10 years before our arrival, one of the two adjacent locks had been closed and filled with rubble so now there was a piece of very rough scrub land between the car park and the still-working lock. The village's main road bridged the canal near this lock and a few hundred yards down the canal there crossed, at right-angles, the only other distinctive feature of the surrounding fields – at this second bridge, a very different mode of transportation raced along over that of an earlier and less hurried age. They were separated only by feet in space but centuries in time. This other distinctive feature was the M6 motorway.

We were entertained, that sunny afternoon, on the small lawn in the garden to the rear of our future home and, as the discussions with the then sub-postmaster and his family progressed, it was obvious that here at last was a place acceptable to all members of the Worthington clan. We bid farewell to our host and retreated to my sister's home to weigh up the pros and cons of this latest possible business venture.

Mum was more enthusiastic than she had been since the start of our quest. She agreed to put up the lion's share of the finance, provided we had the bricks and mortar surveyed, an accountant look at the books and, of course, obtained our own postmaster's approval. In double quick time a contract was drawn up and signed, with clauses allowing us to withdraw should the reports from the surveyor and accountant not prove satisfactory.

Within days, our bungalow was up for sale. Within weeks we had found a buyer. Within months the solicitors began to talk about completion dates.

cHApTEr 7

The two reports from the experts were received and, whilst by no means were they full of advice to 'buy at all costs', they furnished us with enough ammunition to convince Mum to loan us the money we required. To be perfectly honest, we never let Mother have sight of either report but rather conveyed to her only those parts which we believed she would find acceptable. Both the accountant and the surveyor listed the good points. However, they made much of the faults but we believed, with all our recent experiences investigating other properties, that they were hardly worth mentioning.

The surveyor had what seemed to be a very unhealthy interest in the cellar beneath the shop. This cellar, with its wooden ceiling which, of course, was the floor of the shop, was the only cellar in the property. The descent to the cellar was made down a flight of stone steps on which the present owners chose to store the butter, margarine and other fats prior to sale. The shop floor was held up by a couple of beams in size 2 by 2 — that is, not 2"x 2" but 2' x 2'. Their physical appearance was majestic, strong enough to support the weight of the Post Office Tower, but our surveyor was not impressed by appearances. He told us, after only a cursory inspection, that they were riddled with woodworm or was it dry rot or, then again, was it wet rot? Whatever it was our expert was not very keen. We could not but notice that he did not enter the shop again during our visit. I thought he was a little over cautious but, mainly to holster his professional ego, I did not enter the shop again either. The ever-present weight on the shop floor (without customers) was only a large refrigerated display counter, an open-topped display fridge, the Post Office counter and the various other stands and units found in the average village store so what difference would a few extra stones make? (No camels or straw here.) The height of the fall was possibly his reason for not trusting the strength of the supporting beams, and he would have noticed that in the centre of the cellar floor was an open well. This, we had all been told, took the overflow from the nearby Trent and Mersey Canal. We also were shown a small float on the surface of the water in the well, the purpose of this being that, should the level rise, a small pump would automatically switch on to pump any excess water back from whence it came. Whilst finding this arrangement quite amusing, he did not give it or anything else connected with the cellar his seal of approval. His final report, however, was satisfactory for the rest of the property but it was abundantly clear that, unless immediate action was taken, the shop floor with its contents, along with any customers and staff unfortunate enough to be standing on it at the time, were in grave danger of taking an early plunge into the murky waters of the Trent and Mersey Canal overflow.

This part of his report and the section of the accountant's report that said in as many words 'The profits from this business will not support a family of four', though not even denting our desire to purchase, were never shown to Mother.

Everything began to move with increasing speed from then on. Sylvia attended for interview with the Head Postmaster and was appointed Sub-Post Mistress of Hassall Green. The solicitors, having talked for the required time about completion dates, settled on specific days. Unfortunately, the solicitors handling the conveyancing of the bungalow settled for a day which fell five weeks earlier than the day selected by the conveyancing solicitor for the post office. Try as we may, we were unsuccessful in our efforts to make the two dates coincide.

Our problem of the prospect of five homeless weeks was solved very simply by our guardian angels, Glenys and Les. They had a small touring caravan which we borrowed and parked in the third of an acre garden, having obtained permission from the outgoing Postmaster. We also arranged to store our furniture in the empty wood and asbestos lean-to garage and prepared to spend five weeks as gypsies.

During the five weeks, time passed remarkably quickly but, as far as the weather was concerned, we experienced a period of 12 months — or at least all four seasons. Our first week, according to the calendar, was the last week in October of a glorious Indian summer. The days were as hot as June (hotter than the June of that year) and the nights balmy. The second week, the weather cooled, with spells of light rain and slight overnight frost in sheltered places, just like spring or autumn — then came winter. The rain storms were bad but compared favourably when the outside (and the inside of our mobile home) temperature dropped to the side of zero that causes 'brass monkeys' to become soprano. To complete the seasons, we suffered the heaviest snowfall in years. The whole family went down with yet another disease with no known cure — the common cold and, at the stage I had reached with the 'multiples', I preferred it to the common cold.

But, to return to that day in late October in the year of 1968, the day of our move from civilised suburbia to the 'hassle' of Hassall Green. The day dawned. The removal men arrived, packed all our worldly goods into their large van and departed to transport them the 20 odd miles into our new and very different life. I had considered asking Sylvia to travel with and act as navigator to the van driver but, on recalling the occasion of our first 'flit' when she had taken the role of 'pathfinder' and had not only lost the path but the van, driver and mate, along with all the worldly goods. We had only recently acquired, I thought better of it. (On our first move we were moving into an area that Sylvia had not visited before, except the single visit when we viewed the modern semi with three beds etc.) They were missing for four hours on a one-hour journey.

That was our first move, however, and occurred years and years ago. We were now engaged in a third move and were far more experienced. I gave the removal men final instructions, made sure they knew exactly the route they were to take and, with a promise to follow almost immediately, watched them turn the corner at the end of the road. Then I re-entered the bungalow for the last time. Our home for the last four years was now empty, stripped of all indication of those happy years, except for the fitted carpets sold to the new owners who were to take up residency the following day. I walked through the sad rooms in search of Sylvia, who was busy taking down the curtains in the rear bedrooms.

"I've just these and the blue curtains in the lounge to take down, then a quick vac round and we can be off," she said.

"I'll just check round." My reason for doing this last tour was purely sentimental but, not wishing Sylvia to see my emotions, I added, "to make sure that nothing has been left."

I slowly walked through every room again, even into the built-in wardrobe in the main bedroom. In spite of the arrival of the tingles and those other symptoms, the period we had lived at this address had been, in all, as happy a time as any we had known.

Sylvia's voice broke through my melancholy. "If you want to help, collect up the curtains from where I've dropped them, fold them and put them in the car."

"Right-O!" I shouted, thinking, in matters of memory, "Why can't a woman be more like a man."

Before I had put my hands onto the first piece of curtain I heard the vacuum cleaner begin to collect the dust and dirt that my wife believed would have gathered, from heaven knows where, since she had last cleaned the carpets only a few hours earlier.

"What the devil!" I heard her call above the busy noise of the Hoover.

"What, what the devil?" I answered.

"Look to see if you've got anything on your shoes."

I looked. There was still a lot of it on the instep of my right shoe but we were to find most of 'it' thinly dotted on the carpet and, as Sylvia had let the curtains drop to the floor as she removed them from the runners, they too had got a share.

"Why the hell did you throw the curtains on the floor? They're covered too!" I shouted in an effort to put the blame on her.

There then followed one of those shouting matches that normal, rational human beings have at such times. The row lasted throughout the time it took to wash the many spots of soiled carpet and curtain. Every dog owner within a radius of 10 miles took the blame.

"People shouldn't be allowed to have a dog unless they are able to keep it under complete control," I remember declaring.

Within the next months my opinion was to change.

The shouting continued during the journey to re-join our furniture. By the time we reached our destination and drove onto the car park, we saw the doors of the lean-to garage being closed on the majority of our belongings. A large wardrobe, which had proved to be too big for the garage store, had been left standing outside the side door of the main building. We could see that the small caravan that was to be home had been put in position by brother-in-law, Les, who was now assisting in the manoevring of our much-loved furniture. We got out of the car and I walked over to the garage. Opening the doors, I could see the unusual sight of the bottom of our bed settee, fully open, forming an inner door to the garage that only allowed the real wooden garage door to close under pressure. With Les's help the door was forced closed.

"You couldn't get much more in there," I commented.

"You've not seen the half of it," said Les. "We even had to take the light bulb out or we wouldn't have got it all in."

We walked back to where Sylvia stood holding young Jamie, now 18 months old and a little too heavy to hold for long.

"Have you any idea where the pushchair is?" she asked.

I looked to the removal men who were busily closing the van doors and said, "Do you know where the pushchair is?"

The answer, I suppose, was obvious.

"It all depends when it was loaded," said the driver. "Last into the van, first off the van. First off the van, first in the garage."

I looked back to Sylvia. She smiled before she said,

"Oh it definitely was the last thing put onto the van!"

She, as on all such occasions, was correct. The removal men were in the van and away before I could look round, let alone enlist their aid, and so Les and I walked back to the garage. I was more hindrance than help to my sister's husband as we endeavoured to remove the upended bed settee (by this time he must have been doubtful of some of the side effects of holy matrimony). We did manage to move this large obstacle to our progress to the needed pushchair but the task of moving every 'stick' of our furniture seemed overwhelming so, after much thought, Les, with every appearance of Chris Bonnington, began the ascent of the north-west face of Mount Worthington Furniture. In actual fact, it was more of a pothole rescue. He was successful and soon Sylvia, at least, was relieved of the weight of the baby. We persuaded the people still in residence to store our last possession, the wardrobe, in their unused bedroom and so began our five weeks of life in the caravan.

I remember that first evening, at the end of a very warm October, very clearly. With the children bedded down and the turmoil of the day only a memory, Sylvia and I sat with the caravan door wide open, watching the traffic on the near-by motorway race by, and quietly contemplated what our new life style would bring. Apart from the slight tingling in my hands and feet, Multiple Sclerosis belonged to another world.

But to return to the everyday world we must — and did. During the following five weeks our plans were in limbo. I carried on visiting customers' works and offices at all points of my large working area and Sylvia had the difficult task of caring for two children and learning about the running of a village store. (This was not helped by workmen filling in the suspect cellar.) Our boy was the main source of concern; we had been trying for weeks to arrange for an au pair to live with us to give some assistance in this direction but all our efforts had failed to find a suitable young lady. Like innocents in paradise, we kept believing that something would turn up. It did. Sylvia learned from one of her customers that there was a lady living in the village who they felt would be suitable as a child-minder. Whilst we were not very happy about such a casual introduction only 48 hours before the start of our new venture, Sylvia, together with our young and much-loved son walked down the path to knock on the door of Mrs Mary Earn-shaw, who turned out to be someone very special. She became Jamie's second mother and Sylvia's right-hand over the next few years. Agreement was reached that she would commence her duties at 8:30 am on the following Monday.

The contracts and monies changed hands on a Friday lunchtime. As the property and business were now legally ours, we arranged for a heavy gang of friends to attend on Saturday morning to take our furniture from its temporary store and place it in the selected places in our new habitat. A stock-take was carried out on Sunday morning and at 9 o'clock precisely on Monday morning we opened for business and a new era in our life had begun.

cHApTEr 8

We soon settled into our chosen life. Sylvia received training on the ways and duties of a sub-postmistress from an instructor provided by Head Office. This gentleman attended at our sub-office daily for three weeks. Amongst the finer details of everyday transactions and form-filling that Sylvia's position entailed, he worked late on Friday evening to teach her the correct method of bringing the dreaded weekly balance to a successful conclusion.

For the first week of the training, I took a week of my annual holiday to attend to the village store section of our business. The first customer on that first morning was an old fellow who wanted a packet of cigarettes. I thought of Somerset Maughan's story 'The Verger' where, as far as I could remember, the Verger opened a small shop after being forced from his work as the verger at the local church because he was illiterate. After serving his first customer, he took a penny from the money he received from the sale and nailed it to his shop counter as a memento. I considered following the Verger's example, as he went on to make his fortune, but I could not find a hammer, our counter was coated with plastic and was refrigerated and, as I was not sure if my wife and her instructor had read Mr Maughan's story, I decided to spare them the vision of my hammering at the counter. I therefore refused any payment for our first sale, which pleased our first customer but did not lead to a fortune.

I was not sorry when the first week passed. Not only did my disability make me a poor shop assistant in spite of my background, I just did not have the necessary talents. Fortunately, Sylvia did. With her training completed and the man from Head Office from under her feet, she took up her new role and, with very few upsets, managed the 'customer contact' side of our venture with success.

It was a further 12 months before I became, because of my disability, self-employed. During these months, I kept the 'books' of the village store and, on Friday evenings, joined in the shouting and swearing contests that were an integral part of the 'balance'. These contests, which invariably continued into the early hours of Saturday morning without the elusive satisfactory conclusion being reached, on many occasions had barely terminated before the daily early morning delivery of bread and cakes.

I had other tasks to fulfil in our daily life. For instance, every week for two years I roasted a ham for sale in the shop. This service we inherited and I received cooking instructions from our predecessors. Another lesson we had from them was in the twice-weekly visits to the cash-and-carry warehouse. On separate occasions, Sylvia and I accompanied them on this trip when all types of groceries and provisions could be purchased at prices that, at that time, allowed a profit to be made on resale. (Within a short time, and with the advent of the supermarket, this profit was marginal. Within a further short period and with the advent of the hypermarket, the profit was non-existent.) I quite enjoyed this part of our training and so it was decided that I would make the first venture into the wholesale world. I cast my eyes around the shelves, first in the shop and then in the stock room.

"I'm off to C & C now, dear," I called to Sylvia as she attended to her recently returned son (the arrangement with Mary was a success from the very start). "I've had a look round the shop and we appear to be a bit low on pet foods."

"There should be plenty in the stock room. Did you look there?" she asked.

"I looked everywhere. You concentrate on Jamie and getting a meal ready. I'll be about an hour." Then, turning to daughter Jane, I said, "Will you come and help me, love?"

In a flash, Jane was in her coat and at my side, eager to start the mission. This enthusiasm was understandably to wane as the weeks grew into months and the months into years and still the twice-weekly chore remained but, at this time, it was all a great adventure.

"Can we sing, Daddy?"

This became Jane's standard request during the many trips we were to take to the cash and carry.

"Of course, Pet. What do you want to sing?"

This was not to become my standard reply but, whatever my reply was, we sang on all but the rare occasion. 'Where have all the flowers gone' was her first and most popular request during those years before she came under the influence of the Bay City Rollers and the Osmond Brothers. The songs that these people sang I learned to struggle with but, as she progressed(?) to Showaddywaddy, Darts and Mud and even more unlikely-sounding performers (whatever happened to The Animals, The Mindbenders, Dave, Dec Dozy, Beaky, Mozart and Titch, to name but two of the great all-time musicians), I stayed silent.

This first of our musical journeys ended when we reached the warehouse, or at least the location where I had been shown and conducted round the warehouse. All that met our bewildered gaze on that cold December night was a heap of burnt-out rubble that, until two nights earlier, had been 'Williams Brothers' Cash and Carry Warehouse'. I braked to a halt and shouted across the once-busy car park to the small group of men looking at the ruins.

"What's happened? Where's the warehouse gone?"

The men looked at me as if I was a visitor from outer space.

"And where have you been? Don't you watch the telly or read the papers?"

"Not this last week," I answered. "Why?"

"This place was burnt down on Friday night."

Remembering my young daughter's presence — but only just in time, I said, "Flipping heck – I wanted some things for our shop."

"You'll have to go to Queens Street. They've moved down there."

"Thanks," I said, "but where is Queens Street?"

He then gave me complex directions to find the new location of the warehouse, which was almost at the other side of this, to me, unknown town.

Another half hour passed before we located the warehouse. I took my little girl by the hand and led her into the church that had hastily, during the last few days, been converted into a grocery cash and carry (and we thought we had had a traumatic weekend). I collected our usual amount of bacon and then went in search of the pet foods. I found them stacked in the rear corner of a mountain of boxes and tins.

"I want one each of Chappie, Pal, two each of Chum and Bounce and two each of Kit-e-Kat and Whiskers." I ordered from the man in a blue overall who was working amongst the boxes.

"Ten outers all together," he said in acknowledgement of my order.

"No," I said. "I want the full boxes."

The man in the overalls smiled.

"Yes, that's right. We call full boxes outers."

"Of course; yes, 10 outers all together," I said, smiling to cover my ignorance. 'Must remember that,' I thought, but what a stupid name for a full case of tins.

The 10 cases, sorry outers, were loaded onto the trolley alongside the side of bacon I had just collected and we pushed it to the cash-out. I paid for the purchase, which was a few pounds more than the money that we had taken in the shop that day. We could not manage without pet foods, though, so I was not concerned. I helped Jane as much as I was able to load everything into the boot of the car and we drove home, singing all the way.

We arrived a little later than the hour I had suggested to the post mistress, who greeted us with a question.

"Well, what have you bought and how much did it cost?"

"I've got the bacon and 10 ca . . . outers of dog and cat food. I must admit it wasn't cheap but we can't manage without food for the customers' pets."

Sylvia did not appear over impressed with my reasoning.

"Come with me," she said.

I followed her as she walked in a purposeful way into the stock room.

"It's OK. We've got none in there. I looked before we went."

"Did you?" was all she was to say as she walked across the stock room and un-bolted a wooden door, opened it and, with a sweep of her arm, invited me to step into a further little room.

I had seen this door but had never investigated to where it led. I knew from the surveyor's report that it only led to a small lean-to wooden shack known to the previous owners as the 'potting shed' but, as requested, I stepped through the door. Sylvia pointed to a small tier of shelves.

"If you had only looked there before running off to spend all the day's takings you would have seen that we already had two and a half cases of canned pet food."

"You're wrong, my dearest," I said. "I would have seen that we already had two and a half outers of canned pet food. But now I am here to tell you that we have already 12 and a half outers of cans of pet food!"

No more was said on the subject. We had the meal that had been prepared in our absence. I continued in the future to visit the warehouse once every week but from that day forth I was presented with a list of my purchases and woe betide me if I erred from its instructions.

Over the following weeks and months we slowly became organised and evolved a workable system that made our life as pleasant and trouble-free as possible. Jamie seemed no worse for spending five days of every week with his other 'Mum'. It appeared to affect his real mum far more than the boy himself. An arrangement was agreed between his two mums that eased our lives. Mary agreed to stay at the house with Jamie a couple of the five days and, on top of looking after his needs, would do some of Sylvia's neglected housework. We continued our search for an au pair, which we still believed would prove to be the perfect solution to this our main problem.

cHApTEr 9

Another of our concerns, in common with all people who have the responsibility of a sub-post office, was the problem of security. We would read almost every day in the local and national press, reports of daring raids on sub-post offices and villains of all types and all ages were reported gaining entry into any slightly vulnerable office to steal sums of money and stock, varying in value from a few to many thousands of pounds. It was made very clear to us from the beginning that all stock and money in the sub-post office belonged entirely to the Postmaster General; that is until any or all of it was stolen or disappeared in any manner, at which time it became just as completely the property of the sub-postmaster (that is the missing stock or monies).

On one occasion in those early weeks, we believed that a number of insurance stamps had been stolen. Our suspicions were confirmed during the following Friday balance – we were approximately £70 'down'. We obeyed the rules as laid down in the large manual of instructions Sylvia had been presented with and reported the discrepancy to Head Office. They were very understanding, refusing our offer to make good 'our' stock in seven weekly payments of £10.

"Oh no, that's not on!" the man from Head Office said. "Far too much. Fourteen weekly payments of £5 will be sufficient."

This action by the Post Office authorities is no doubt justifiable, as we also heard of great amounts going 'missing' with or without the knowledge of the sub-post-office staff. There was that memorable case in 1963 when some poor unfortunate Post Office employee had the misfortune to be robbed of £2,500,000 from his travelling Post Office. Now, this type of theft may never have been attempted before. When the villains were caught they were charged with stealing this vast amount, not from the Postmaster General, but from the senior Post Office employee in charge of that infamous train. If he received the same treatment on 'his' loss of £2,500,000 as we did on 'our' loss of £70, it's a wonder he did not joins Biggsy in Argentina. Or, then again, for all we know he may still be paying it off at £10,000 a week!

We had a couple of visits from the criminal classes but this was not until a few years later so, in the interests of chronology, the telling must wait. My mother and one or two of our more nervous friends were not surprised when eventually we were 'hit'. They had pointed out to us on many occasions that the M6 Motorway was only a field away and so, therefore, London with the Krays, Richardsons and the like was within a couple of hours hard drive in a 'souped-up' get-away car. Their fears impressed us even less, I am sure, than the possible easy pickings at Hassall Green Post Office impressed the gangsters in our capital city.

In deference to these views, it was decided that we should have a guard dog. In the spring of our first year in residence we were informed that on the edge of the village lived a couple who had a business specialising in breeding Alsatians. We visited their kennels (I use this word in its loosest meaning). We were told they lived in quite a large detached house but we found, on arrival, that the dogs lived in quite a large detached house. Where the couple lived we were never to discover. The place should have been visited by an old school teacher of mine who, given the least cause, would twitch his nose and say, "There is a nauseating aroma prevalent," so causing the young person who was the source of the nauseating aroma much embarrassment. The aroma of these 'kennels', dogs and breeders would have been the death of my old teacher. This nauseating aroma was of Olympic standard. With a smell like this, who needed a guard dog?

We did not stay long. Just long enough to ask if they had a good dog for sale.

"No, not at the moment," the male breeder said. "But we have a bitch due to have puppies this week. If you wish, we could let you have one of those."

"You wouldn't be able to take it for a couple of months, of course," said the female member of the firm.

"That's OK," I called from the end of the road where Sylvia and I had retreated, where the air was clearer.

Only a week had passed when I answered a knock on our side door. I was not surprised, on opening it, to find the lady dog breeder standing there. The smell could and had with ease permeated through our sturdy door.

"We have a dog you can have if you like," she began. "It's one we sold to a man in Chester about six months ago as a puppy but he brought it back this morning as he thinks it has grown too big for him."

"Could we have it today?" I asked.

Not that I was in a terrible rush to have the animal but the shorter the time it had to be in those foul-smelling 'kennels' the better.

"I can bring it right away if you are interested," she offered.

"If you could do that we would be pleased."

With that, I closed the door as politely but as quickly as possible, gasping for fresh air as I did.

I went back into our sweet-smelling home and informed the family of the arrangement I had made. Half an hour later there was another knock at the door. Sylvia answered this time and led the lady breeder and a beautiful tan and brown Alsatian dog into our living room. It really was a perfect specimen. The dog was very quiet and friendly and the whole family, even two-year old Jamie, were soon fussing over this large animal as it nuzzled us each in turn with its cold, wet nose. Under this nose we would see a very full and vicious looking mouthful of teeth but the dog showed not even a minor amount of aggression.

"There is no need to be afraid of him," said the lady. "He is a big baby really — very good with children."

"Yes," said Sylvia. "He certainly is fine with these two. How much will he cost us?"

"Well, as I told your husband, we've had him returned by a customer because he's grown so big but don't let that worry you. No matter how big they grow they are just like babies." As she was saying this, she grabbed hold of the dog and dragged him onto her lap and began to love and kiss the apparently willing animal. "If you give them lots of love, they will love you in return."

"I can see that, but how much?" As an animal lover, I wanted to rescue the poor animal from the fate worse than death it was being subjected to.

"Well it should be £25 but, as it's second-hand, you can have him for £15."

"£15? OK, we'll have him."

I reached for the cheque book as, at that time, MS had not reached to the nerves that controlled my hands, so causing my handwriting to deteriorate into an undecipherable scrawl.

"£15 15s 0d and could you let me have cash please?" our visitor said very quickly.

The lady departed with the cash, leaving us with 'Kim', the latest addition to the family.

"Doesn't he smell!" said our elder child.

"Yes, he does." agreed Sylvia. "Bob, do you think you can manage to give him a bath?"

The dog followed me upstairs into the bathroom with no trouble. I closed the bathroom door to cut off any means of retreat for Kim and filled the bath with warm water; then came the difficult bit. Kim was a big dog; his weight could not have been very much less than mine, at least it did not feel so when I tried to lift him to drop him into the water. As soon as the friendly dog realised what my intentions were he became less friendly. I was to discover within the following 15 to 20 minutes two things. Firstly, I discovered how much my disease had affected my balance and strength. I did in the end succeed in getting the dog into the bath but not before we had both rolled around the floor like two engaged in a bout of 'catch-as-catch-can' wrestling and even my prize of seeing the dog in the bath was marred as there was little water in the bath, most of it was on the bathroom floor, and I was in there with him. The rest of the family came running up the stairs to find the cause of all the noise and very unfeelingly laughed. The second thing I discovered in those minutes concerned the dog's character. It was a coward. At least it would not fight, fortunately for me. That evening, if it had been the type of dog with any fight in it, it would have torn me to pieces.

However, I was assisted out of the bath and the family completed the animal's ablutions whilst I dried myself and changed into dry clothes. We returned to the living room and we found a home for two tins from the six 'outers' that I had bought six months ago. (We did not sell much dog food!) We sat around the fire watching the children play with our 'guard dog' for an hour before their mother announced that bedtime had arrived. Whilst Sylvia attended to our offspring, I watched the "box" and Kim curled up to recover from the contest of the bathroom. Sylvia re-joined me and, for the first time since we moved, we sat down together to enjoy a couple of hours of television.

Around half past ten that evening I turned to Sylvia.

"If you'll make us some coffee, I'll take Kim for a walk."

"No, you make the coffee and I'll take Kim for a walk. My legs are healthier than yours," she suggested.

"No love," I argued. "You make the coffee. I want to take the dog to prove to him that there are no hard feelings after our fight."

Sylvia put up no further objection so I put on Kim the short lead that had been given to us with the dog and led him through the side door and onto the car park. In the months that we had been in residence I had not had the desire, time or ability to explore the immediate external surroundings of our home. I knew of the canal and the filled-in lock but had never walked onto the rough ground between the car park and the working lock and so it was with extreme caution that I led the dog onto this piece of scrubland. It was a dark night so I had no intention of going anywhere near the lock or canal. I could see the flags that marked the edge of the now unused and earth-filled old lock. I walked along this comparatively smooth surface towards the village road bridge. Kim walked calmly at my side at the only distance that his short lead would allow. I had reached a point about five yards from the bridge and I looked down to see if the surface of the earth filling the lock was level enough not to trip up my unsteady motion. I was surprised to see a smooth black surface to the side of me. The thought flashed through my mind that the Waterways Board had laid tarmacadam over this piece of land to give canal users at least a little stretch of firm level surface. So, giving the lead a small tug and saying, "Come on boy," I took a smooth step onto the tarmac. At that precise moment I learnt how perfectly true the saying 'falling head first' is. I know it is to do with the centre of gravity of a human frame being high in the torso so that should any human be stupid enough to step into space, as I did then, his head will very quickly take up a position such that it will meet any obstacle in its path before his feet. That night I found that the whole of this applies equally to man's best friend, the dog.

I suppose it could be said that I had a choice in taking that step into space but not Kim. I plunged down onto the slope that had resulted from the contractors who had filled in the lock being short of filling material when they reached a point approximately eight yards from the road bridge, Kim following me as I firmly held on to his lead. We landed in a heap on the slope. Neither of us had more than slight bruises but that evening must have put understanding between man and dog back light years.

We helped each other back through the black night, up the slope the longer but safer way, and back across the car park where not only did the ground look like tarmacadam, it was tarmacadam.

Over the ensuing weeks I came to find that my first assessment of the dog's character was accurate. He did not have the necessary qualities to be a guard dog. The philosophy was 'the dog who only nips and bays lives to fight on other days'. It was damned embarrassing. If he was on the lead or restrained in any way he would, with almost no provocation, give a display of aggressive barking and growling that would have put the Hound of the Baskervilles to shame and even this was mainly reserved for small children and little old ladies. He had a nasty habit, should he get out-of-doors unattended, of giving the display to anyone who ventured onto the car park — and all our customers fell into this category. As I say, the display was all show but who would blame even the bravest mortal, when faced with a large, snarling Alsatian, should they beat a hasty retreat. The first refuge for these stricken souls was the telephone box. This proved to be a very safe sanctuary during Kim's reign. Its main drawback appeared, if the dog had been at large a length of time, when the fleeing person had a chance of finding the telephone box overcrowded with subjects of the dog's previous attentions. After this had happened a number of times and, if Sylvia had not had a customer for around 20 minutes, she would first check if the guard dog was safely indoors and, if it was not, she would rescue any prisoner from the telephone box. We may possibly have lost some custom due to the dog but there was a fair chance of gaining customers from people who, setting out for a stroll or healthy brisk walk, fell into the jaws of our customer collector.

During daylight hours the term of confinement in the telephone box was limited to a matter of minutes. However, after darkness fell, the sentence could be extensive. We were aware and worried about this definite possibility and so, after some consideration, we placed a notice in the kiosk simply saying 'If a large dog has you trapped, please phone (transfer charges)' and to this we added our telephone number. We received no complaints from rescued people. This, I believe, was because of embarrassment on their part on finding that the dog was as timid as a mouse.

We decided that, nonetheless, should Kim's habits not be corrected, the number of complaints would soon begin so, after seeing a programme on the box on dog obedience, I decided to train our guard dog. Kim's stay with us was only to last a matter of weeks. An incident in one of our early training sessions hastened his departure.

cHApTEr 10

Kim's first lessons in obedience were given indoors and the progress was unbelievably good. He would sit to command and remain sitting whilst I walked around the room so, encouraged by this success, I decided to give all further lessons in the great outdoors.

The next Sunday afternoon found the weather warm and sunny. I attached the dog to the end of a long lead and took him, a rubber ball and a box of 'Doggychocs' into the front garden. The garden, mainly lawn, was situated between the house and the road and was the longest stretch of land we owned. The canal and car park were at the shorter end of the lawn, separated by a not very sturdy wooden fence. The other end had no clear boundary. It just petered out in a tangled mass of nettles, tall grass, lawn and hedge cuttings and other debris which are usually found at the end of an English country garden. Most of the garden refuse in this tangled mass came from the hawthorn hedge that separated the garden from the road running past the front of our domain, from the canal bridge into the centre of our village. The whole garden was approximately 15 yards by 35 yards; not a very big area but quite big enough to teach the dog the basics of sit, lie and fetch obedience, which was all I wished to teach the dog in this lesson. The more complex lessons of seize and kill would have to wait until the following Sunday.

I very quickly had Kim retrieving the ball, sitting and lying to command. I had only rewarded him with half the box of 'Doggychocs' and so, with complete confidence, I progressed to the next stage of my carefully-planned training programme. The ultimate test — I unclipped the lead. I cannot stress how big a step this was. In the past, if Kim had gained his freedom he did not give it up until the next mealtime. But, on this occasion, Kim did not 'bolt'; he remained seated whilst I walked backwards a few yards — well, if not a few yards, a few feet. I called to him and he came. I was overcome with a wave of emotion at this success. I picked up the ball and threw it to the other end of the garden near the car park. Kim gave a mystified look and was after it like a train. He gathered the ball on its first bounce, spun around and, at my command of 'sit', he sat. Tears welled up in my eyes — man and dog were one.

My euphoria was short-lived for, over the dog's head, I could see a young couple, hand-in-hand, walking towards the road from the direction of the canal. 'Love's young dream on a sunny Sunday afternoon walk along the canal towpath,' I thought. Kim was completely unaware of their presence but I was very aware that in a matter of seconds they would only be a few yards from him. The couple were dressed in identical blue jeans and sweaters — what I believe are called unisex clothes. This type of clothing should be described as unisex before it adorns the human frame and, even then, I will concede that there are certain female frames which, when dressed in this type of apparel, can, to the untrained eye, appear male and *vice versa*. Then, none of us are perfect; but, as a fully paid-up, card carrying member of the 'Vive la Difference' Society, 10 times out of 10 I can tell. However, with this particular couple, even a novice would have had no trouble in 'finding the lady'. He was lean of hip and she was lean of nowhere — not front, top nor rear lower. It was this rear lower section of the lady's anatomy which was to appeal to Kim's canine nature when, as soon as he was aware of their presence, what I had feared came to pass. The newly found understanding between man and beast proved to be as brittle as thin glass.

I struggled to reach the scene of the impending action, shouting my full range of commands in rapid succession. I had difficulty moving but not so Kim. With one silent leap he was over the hedge, up behind the couple, in, nip, and away. The young chap didn't know what was happening but his girlfriend did. I can still hear the 'ring' of her maidenly voice as it came over on the clear air that beautiful, sunny afternoon in those beautiful rural surroundings.

"Bloody hell! That dog's bitten me bum!" she screamed.

I stopped in mid-stagger. "I'm very sorry but I didn't order him to do that," I said in apology.

She looked to her companion for assistance but he, sensible fellow, had calmly dropped her hand and was quietly carrying on with his walk. I will say this for the girl, she had the situation weighed up very quickly.

"He's not got that dog under control," she shouted after her friend, completely ignoring my apology.

The boyfriend continued walking without so much as a glance backwards. Kim, true to character, had returned to the safety of the garden. He must have been satisfied with the nip as he sat in front of me, allowing me to return him to the lead. The girl, after making more unpleasant comments about me and my dog, ran after her disappearing friend, catching him up about 50 yards past the end of our property. Even from this distance I could hear the better or worse part of their shouted conversation which ended with the girl taunting her partner.

"Go on then — go back and thump him!"

I saw the man stop and take a pace in my direction to where I still stood defiantly restraining the Alsatian who, now very secure on the lead, was giving his best impression of a mentally-deranged sabre-toothed tiger. 'Romeo' hesitated, put his arm round the girl's shoulder and led her further along the road, away from the reunited man and dog.

Sylvia appeared through the front door and joined Kim and I on the lawn. She admitted that she had been observing the scene from behind the curtains of an upstairs window.

"You could have come out and given me moral support," I complained.

"That wouldn't have helped," she said. "The girl was speaking the truth when she said the dog wasn't under control. Why don't you admit that the dog is too big and we haven't got time to train it?"

"I was doing great before Adam and Eve came along. Another couple of sessions and I'll have him eating out of my hand," I answered.

Oh why oh why can't a woman be more like a man – or even a dog?

"He can eat out of your hand now. The only trouble is what he's eating."

There then followed a discussion reminiscent of our Friday nights. The outcome was a telephone call I made the following day to the Headquarters of the Cheshire Constabulary who I understood wanted dogs to train as police dogs.

The police were very grateful for the offer and I made arrangements for them to visit us one day of the following week to assess Kim's potential.

I was out when they did call on the following Thursday but I received a full and detailed report from my wife.

"Well, what did they think of him?" I asked Sylvia when I returned home that evening.

"The policeman who came didn't give a final decision. He said he would bring his sergeant to see Kim on Saturday morning."

"I bet he was impressed with him though," I commented.

"Well, he didn't say," Sylvia said. "He seemed impressed but he only looked through the window. Not that I blamed him as Kim was at his fiercest, barking and growling. It's a wonder he didn't uproot the pole." (During the day we had taken to trying him to a post in the back garden at the end of a short length of thick rope.)

"Oh, they'll have him all right. They know a good dog when they see one and when they complete my training of him, he'll make a first-class police dog. Then you'll be sorry I decided not to complete his training," I retaliated.

On the Saturday morning I had Kim outside, tied to the pole, ready for his in-spection by the guardians of the law. I was afraid that the animal would not give his best display of aggression but I need not have worried. As soon as I appeared with the two policemen at our kitchen window we were witnesses to a sight that I was sure would terrify even the bravest lion tamer. The sergeant in charge of training police dogs in Cheshire spoke,

"You've certainly got a beautiful dog there."

"Yes," I agreed. "But I'm afraid he's just a bit too much for us to handle. It's the wife really — she doesn't understand animals so that's the reason I have decided to let you have him."

"He certainly is a handsome animal. Shall we go and have a closer look at him?" said the sergeant.

"Yes. That'll be all right; as long as you're with me you'll be quite safe," I informed him.

We went through the back door into the garden. Kim increased the noise by a few decibels and I glanced at the officers who seemed impressed with the dog's performance.

"How long have you had him?" asked the constable.

"Only a couple of months," I answered. "But he's nearly 12 months old."

I then noticed that, as we talked, the two policemen, with hands deep in the pockets of their regulation raincoats, were very slowly inching towards the dog and its slavering jaws. I was about to warn them of the danger they were moving into when I further noticed that, whilst Kim kept up his savage noises, the rope holding him was no longer taut. I watched and, as the policemen advanced, the rope became slacker and slacker. Suddenly the sergeant, with a quick movement of his hands, flapped the tails of his raincoat. His movement caused me to start a little but the effect on Kim was unbelievable. He emptied his bowels as he made a perfect somersault and, once more, the rope was taut as he tried to make a howling get-away over the garden fence.

The two policemen, with only a sharp look at each other, turned and gave me a pleasant but sad look. There was no need for any remarks but the sergeant said,

"Have you ever thought of showing Kim? He's a fine animal."

"By that I take it you don't want him?"

"Well, Mr Worthington, he's just a little bit on the timid side. Not quite the type of dog we require. You see, we want our dogs to 'go in' and get a man with a club or gun. It looks as if your dog is vicious but he isn't."

I was tempted to ask if they ever got any old ladies, not wearing raincoats, who they wanted rounding up into a telephone box but I decided against it.

They went after giving us their thanks for our kind offer and I went to tranquilise the terrified dog. He suffered no ill effects from his police inspection. Within two hours of its completion, he 'escaped' and very quickly had a man, two women and two stray cats imprisoned in the kiosk.

Further conferences were held to discuss Kim's future and decisions were taken to put advertisements in the local press in order to find a good home for our discharged guard dog. These appeared in print a few days later and a very good home was found for Kim. His new owners brought him to visit us a couple of months later. The whole family were pleased to see him in good health but were a little sorry to find that he obviously did not remember any of us.

None of the family could honestly say they missed Kim as, by the time of this visit, another dog had taken his place. Not as a guard dog, however, just as a family pet. Kim's successor was a Golden Labrador named Sasha. He was presented to us by friends who, having followed Kim's stay with us very closely and on hearing that he had gone to pastures new, gave Sasha to us to heal any broken hearts. The arrival of our second dog coincided with another arrival but this one we had hoped and searched for during the better part of 12 months. Some 10 months later than planned, we had an au pair.

cHApTEr 11

Whilst Mary was proving to be an efficient and loving child-minder, we continued our efforts to obtain an au pair to take care of our son. We felt that this would be a better arrangement inasmuch that Jamie would still feel a full-time member of the family rather than someone collected on five mornings in every seven and taken to spend the day in the company of a person from outside his family.

After many weeks, arrangements were made with the assistance of a friend's au pair. A young Spanish girl would arrive at Manchester Airport to take up the position of 'nanny' for our boy.

So began a very traumatic period for one and all. The first evening was quite pleasant on the whole with only one pointer to the unsettling future.

We met Marta (for that was her name) at the airport and we drove her 15 miles to what was intended to be her home for the next 12 months. We did our utmost to make her welcome. She was introduced to her ward and his sister and they appeared to take to each other immediately. In spite of any language barrier, Jane had them singing 'Where have all the flowers gone' before the journey home was a couple of miles old.

On arrival at our home, Marta was shown her room; the only room in the house that we had decorated since taking up residence. All the family (in fact, this was the last decorating my disability permitted me to do.) had spent every spare moment in the week prior to Marta's arrival with paint, brush, wallpaper and other tools of the 'do-it-yourself' home decorator. We had bought a new bed, curtains and carpet, hoping that our au pair would not feel under-privileged. She, I believe, was suitably impressed with the result of our toil as we were with her generosity when she presented Sylvia with a quart bottle of Bacardi and me with a box of 25 very good cigars.

After a cup of coffee, we decided to have an early night but, before retiring to bed, I thought it best to telephone Mum and let her know of the au pair's safe arrival. From the very beginning, Mum had not been 100% certain that she should allow her only grandson to be left in the care of any Spaniard, unless they could provide absolute proof that, if not they themselves, then all their ancestors had been active members of the 'International Brigade'[7]. I dialled Mum's number and, when she answered, I informed her of Marta's arrival. I wanted to say goodnight then but Mum insisted on speaking to our young visitor. With some trepidation I handed the telephone to the young girl who was incapable of putting more than a couple of words together in the only language my mum knew. Marta put the instrument to her ear and listened for a short time; then she began to chatter into the telephone in her native tongue. Before I had time to look at Sylvia, who was as baffled as I was at Mum's sudden linguistic prowess, Marta burst into heart-rending tears. I quickly took the telephone from Marta as I glanced at my shattered family who were actively endeavouring to console the distraught Spanish girl.

"What the hell did you say?" I screamed down the mouthpiece to my mother.

"Only – mi casa es su casa."

"What does that mean?" I asked, watching Sylvia sooth the sobbing girl.

"Oh, I don't know what it means. At least, I'm not sure," confessed Mum. "I heard it on 'High Chaparral' on the television last week."

"Brilliant!" I shouted rudely. "Haven't you any idea what it means?"

"No idea," she said, completely unaware of the effect her words had had on our new au pair. "Why don't you ask her?"

---

7 Military units made up of volunteers from different countries who travelled to Spain to fight for the Second Spanish Republic in the Spanish Civil War.

Happily, I declined as it may have spoiled Marta's pleasure for we were to discover the translation of Mum's attempt at Spanish a few days later. It was an old Spanish greeting. Marta's tears were tears of happiness on being given a welcome in her mother tongue. Knowing the source of my mother's quotation, we were lucky that the translation was not 'Strap on your side irons, this town isn't big enough for the both of us' or, remembering the language used in some of television's more popular shows, it might have been even worse. The mind boggles.

I said goodnight to Mother, hung up the telephone and herded the two children to their beds whilst Sylvia gave all her attention to settling a now smiling Marta. The house was soon in darkness with all the inhabitants, if not sound asleep, in various degrees of exhausted silence. The following day being Sunday would allow us the time to get better acquainted with our au pair.

Marta was perhaps a little heavy and ungainly when compared to the 'skinny birds' currently in modern day fashion. She was nonetheless a pretty and attractive girl. During that first day (in fact during the whole of her time with us) the children appeared to have no difficulty in communicating with her and were very soon teaching her songs and learning songs from her. The previous evening's tears were a thing of the past and we were one big, happy family. Marta used Christian names when speaking to the children and Sylvia but she insisted on calling me 'Mester Worthinkton'. Sylvia's name gave her a little difficulty but her version, 'Seelvea', was recognisable.

After quite a peaceful day and with the two younger members safely tucked up in bed, the three older members sat down to discuss, in more detail, future arrangements in our new circumstances. I gave Marta her first English money, making it way in excess of the going rate for au pairs. Also, we decided that Mary would have Jamie for one more week, giving Marta time to become familiar with her new surroundings. It would also allow time for Marta to be registered with the local police and to be introduced to the local priest, as she was a practising Roman Catholic. With these matters settled, Sylvia went into the kitchen to make coffee. Immediately, Marta rose and followed her, insisting that she must relieve Sylvia of this task. As well, she went on to inform Sylvia that, as she enjoyed cooking, she would be pleased if we would allow her to prepare some of our meals. You must realise that this exchange of information was only possible with much mime, pointing and arm-waving. Sylvia and I were delighted at this unexpected bonus to the arrangements and agreed without any further discussions. In fact, Sylvia proceeded at one to show Marta our method of making the evening beverages. She demonstrated how we mixed an equal amount of milk and water and, after heating, poured the hot liquid into mugs, each having one teaspoonful of coffee powder. Marta mastered this procedure perfectly. She did, however, misunderstand Sylvia's instructions on one point; she now believed that every drop of milk that came into the house was to be mixed with an equal amount of water and no amount of miming and arm-waving would shake her belief.

After a few mornings, the family learned to arise much earlier, hoping to rescue the milk for their cereals. At least the problem, experienced by many families, of early morning rising was solved for us. The late risers found they were faced with watery milk on their cornflakes. This benefit was not to last, however, as the following week the milkman changed the time of his delivery from early morning to later in the day, when Sylvia could not guard it from the attentions of Marta. It also gave us a few minutes more in the mornings whilst Marta recovered the milk from the shop refrigerator to change it from its natural state. Before we could become accustomed to real milk on the cornflakes, Marta politely requested permission to retire to bed much later than us as her lifestyle in Spain included only a few hours of night-time sleep. We, of course, agreed. We should have known better. She was now left alone with the milk! We would descend the stairs each morning and, in the kitchen, find every jug and bowl we possessed full to the brim with 'Spanish milk'. We endeavoured in all manners to break Marta's belief in our treatment of milk and, in a last desperate effort before leaving her to go to bed, I collected a bottle of undiluted milk, held it up in front of Marta and, with an exaggerated shaking of my head, I shouted

"No!"

I felt sure that she must have got the message. That is until, as I climbed the stairs with my wife (who had watched my performance in silence), Sylvia looked at me, gave me a sweet smile and said,

"Don't worry darling, I think you made it clear that you don't want her to forget to mix the milk!"

The following morning, the pints and pints of milk and water proved Sylvia's interpretation of my pantomime had matched Marta's. Eventually, we found the only positive solution to the problem. We went to bed carrying bottles of hot water and separate bottles of cold milk.

Of all the meals that Marta prepared for us, torte and paella were our favourites. They more than compensated for having to store bottles of milk under our beds. However, soon we were to learn of another of Marta's habits.

On most evenings, after Sylvia and I had completed the many necessary small tasks essential in running a village store (the least popular of which was the re-stocking of the shelves in preparation for the next day's customers) we would sit to relax with a cup of coffee. The coffee, made and served by our au pair, was always to our liking. Then our total enjoyment would be spoiled when Marta would appear from the kitchen with an empty tray to walk briskly through the room and into the shop. She would reappear after a few minutes with the tray overflowing with pounds (sterling) worth of many different types of foodstuffs. She carried on this transfer of the stock from the shop to the kitchen shelves almost every night. We would smile at each other and then at this sweet Spanish girl but would remain silent. We had come to realise in the first week that the language barrier, if not insurmountable, was eased by acknowledging its presence and taking action to avoid speech. So, on these occasions, we just hoped that Marta was not in the process of stocking a shop to open in opposition to us and we would, at the next opportune moment, reverse the flow of saleable goods. Marta did not appear to notice that her efforts were not increasing the amount of food on the kitchen shelves but she did increase the quantity on her tray.

Marta soon settled into her new life. She was very independent and quickly made a couple of friends of her own age in the village. One day, we were surprised and concerned to learn from her that she had paid a visit to the nearest city, Manchester. She excitedly told us of a man she had met who had insisted in taking her into one of the city's wine bars (the mimes that accompanied this transfer of information left little to our imagination). Marta's adventure in the city so much affected Sylvia's maternal instinct that on the following day she visited the Catholic church that Marta attended to enlist the help of the priest. She told him of Marta's wanderings and of how worried she was about the girl's welfare.

"I understand your concern, Mrs Worthington, and I am sure it must be a comfort to the girl's family knowing of your interest in Marta's wellbeing," said the Priest.

"Thank you, Father," said a relieved Sylvia. "I would feel happier if you would have a word with her about the — er — possible dangers if she — er — wanders."

"Now don't you worry any more, Mrs Worthington. You have done your duty," said Marta's spiritual father. "I will see Marta on Sunday at Mass and I will take full responsibility for her welfare."

The next Sunday, Marta arrived home from her weekly worship and requested that she be allowed to have the following Wednesday 'off' as the priest wished her to spend the day with him. With this news, Sylvia's maternal concern was totally satisfied. She made the necessary arrangements for the care of Jamie, informed Marta that she could have the day off with pleasure and with much difficulty told her she hoped she would have a pleasant day's break. My wife was now full of praise for the whole Catholic Church but especially for our local parish priest, for the obvious care they took of their flock and the speed with which they took up their responsibilities to them. Her newly found faith was put to its first test the next Wednesday.

It proved to be hot and sunny that day when, at 10.30 in the morning, there raced onto our car park a brightly coloured sports car. With screaming tyres it came to a halt amid clouds of dust and smoke from burning rubber. Out of the driving seat leapt a tanned young man, dressed in the very latest 'with it' clothes — expensive slacks and a pure white roll-necked sweater. Yes, this was Marta's parish priest! He bounced into the shop, was immediately joined by our au pair, and they ran back to the 'wheels'. Waiting in the cramped rear seat was another similarly dressed young man, the only major difference being that this young man was already 'kitted up' with a beautiful 'dolly bird' nestling at his side. With the engine at maximum revolutions, the car made a scorching exit from the confines of Hassall Green Post Office and Village Store.

"He's changed almost beyond recognition since Sunday," claimed Sylvia. "He didn't look a bit like that when I called him 'Father'."

"Well, Marta certainly recognised him," I said. "Are you sure he's not advertising Martini or Pirelli tyres of something?"

We never came to know if Marta's 'Father' had a 'day job' with some glamorous advertising agency but his attentions met with her full approval as the trip became a weekly event during Marta's stay with us.

cHApTEr 12

Sylvia and I were now able to make the twice-weekly trips to the cash and carry warehouse together whilst Marta attended to the children. The two visits of the first week proved very successful; we returned home to find both Jane and Jamie safely and happily washed and tucked up in bed. Sylvia and I unloaded the purchases we had made at the warehouse (not one tin of pet food) and, on completion, found that Marta had prepared a meal for us. Now here was the good life!

We prepared to make the first visit of Marta's second week with us. We made a list of requirements, ensuring that we had sufficient money for the purchases, and departed with a promise from Marta.

"When you return the children are in bed and good food baked."

This was a great improvement in Marta's attempts to communicate, since only two days earlier her morning greeting, after a rather stormy night, was the legendary,

"Seelvea, I have much wind today!"

We completed our business at the cash and carry very quickly that evening and so called for a drink at one of the local pubs on our journey home. This was one of the many things that had been missing from our way of life since our entrance into the world of sub-post offices and village stores. We enjoyed the liquid refreshment and discussed the possible culinary delight that would be awaiting our pleasure back at 'the ranch'. We drove onto the car park, sniffing the early summer evening air, hoping to get a hint of the nature of our eagerly-awaited meal. It was not our nostrils that were excited, however, it was our eyes. The shop door was wide open.

We got out of the car, all thoughts of food gone. By the time I had managed to transport myself into the shop, I could hear Sylvia running through the kitchen, calling for Marta. By the time I had managed to get to the kitchen, I could hear Sylvia running up the stairs, shouting for Marta. By the time I had reached the foot of the stairs, Sylvia was on her way down, screaming for Marta.

"Now calm down," I shouted. "She's probably taken the kids into the garden."

"Oh, the kids are in bed. It's only Marta who's disappeared," she said, a little calmer as the realisation of the children's safety sank in.

"Now don't worry, and for God's sake slow down. With the shop door wide open she won't be far away. You go and 'panic' in the front garden and I'll have a look round the back."

We separated as I had suggested, both calling for our au pair but with no response from the young Spanish girl. We met on the car park outside the still-open shop door. Around five minutes had passed since we had driven back to the deserted premises. I walked from the car park onto the canal bank and glanced upstream to the point, some few hundred yards distant, where the canal disappeared from view around a bend in its route. As I looked, around the bend strolled our au pair accompanied by one of the girls from the village.

"She's coming along the tow path," I called to Sylvia as I waved and beckoned to Marta.

My attempts at communication met with the same success at hundreds of yards as it did at a few feet. Sylvia joined me on the canal bank and we waited the few minutes until the two girls reached us. Sylvia began to remonstrate as the four of us walked back to the shop. Her efforts of conveying to Marta the importance of never leaving the premises unattended, let alone leaving it with the main entrance gaping, were met with blank incomprehension. So, without waiting for the usual call of 'Beginners please,' Sylvia began a performance of a little-known work entitled 'Robbery in the Village Store'. In true Tom and Jerry fashion, she crouched and crept on tiptoe into the empty shop, she went to empty the till but remembered, on opening it, that we had just spent its last contents at the warehouse. She then collected as many packets of cigarettes she could find and, collecting one medium can of Heinz beans, she made her exit, still creeping, back onto the car park. I had stood back with the two girls throughout the performance and now, suppressing an overwhelming desire to applaud at its completion, I waited for the reaction of the other members of the small audience. There was total silence. I am fairly confident that the village girl understood the message contained in Sylvia's acting but it was beyond any shadow of doubt that the whole performance (of which I will be amongst the first to admit it had some weak points — the full significance of the tin of baked beans still escapes me) was not fully appreciated or understood by that member of the audience at whom it was aimed. Sylvia refused to perform again. Instead, taking Marta by the arm, she all but dragged her into the shop and, making great play, she locked and bolted the offending door.

The local girl and I were on the car park side of the door but Sylvia's voice reached us with only minor attenuation.

"Lock door. No want thief. No burglar manana, gracias!"

I realised that Sylvia had broken the barrier when I heard Marta say,

"Oh no, Seelvea, not theeves. Not in England!"

There was only a small pause before the shop door was opened by a smiling Marta. As she stepped through the doorway, she turned to Sylvia.

"I go for walk today. You discover food in cooker," and with that she walked towards the canal with the unbelieving English girl following.

"Now mind you don't fall in," I called after them, keeping a sharp eye on Sylvia in case she made any ominous move towards the canal and Marta.

"Come on love," I said to Sylvia. "Let's go and have our exotic meal. You'll feel much better after paella or some such. We'll open a bottle of wine and pretend we are on the Costa Brava again."

We went into the kitchen and I opened the oven door with watering mouth. What I saw there dried my mouth quicker than sucking an old penny. Our meal was to be that old Spanish delicacy 'Cod ball and chips' direct from our freezer in the shop!

A few days later, everything was forgotten and forgiven on all sides. Peace returned for a while until Sylvia was reminded of the one piece of furniture that we had not placed in Marta's room when Marta approached her carrying an old wooden chair, mimed painting the chair and the making of a cushion for it. My wife had mastered the sign language to such a degree that she realised Marta wished to paint the chair and make a cushion for it.

"Yes Marta," she said with much nodding of her head. "I will find you a brush and some paint."

Rather than mime the last part of her answer, Sylvia quickly found the needed items.

"Here you are, Marta. You can have these. Please paint (brushing actions) on the back lawn (pointing through kitchen window). Take Jamie (pointing to the boy) with you (pointing to Marta); the fresh air will do him good." (This remark she felt was beyond mime so she kissed Jamie and returned to her customers in the shop).

After attending to the customers, Sylvia returned to the kitchen and, through the window, she could see Marta busily painting whilst Jamie played at her side. Almost an hour passed before there was another 'lull' in trade, when Jamie's Mum had the opportunity to check Marta's progress in furniture renovation. She was surprised, on entering the kitchen, to find her son sitting on the edge of the sink whilst Marta, holding him securely with one arm, wiped the inside of his mouth with a wet cloth held in her free hand. The boy did not like it — but then neither did his Mum.

"What's the matter," shouted Sylvia, rushing over to rescue her son.

Marta burst forth into rapid Spanish which conveyed nothing to Jamie's anxious mother. However, as soon as the miming began, the sequence of events that had led up to Sylvia's appearance in the kitchen became clear. The mime consisted of Marta picking up the paint brush, dripping Dulux brilliant white paint in various amounts on the sink, draining board, kitchen floor and, not least of all, on James Leslie (luckily not a drop went on Marta), close to the small boy's mouth. She then picked up a bottle from the side of Jamie, poured some of its contents onto the cloth and continued her explanation by cleaning inside his mouth. He still did not like it!

Sylvia made a grab for the bottle, took one look at the word 'TURPENTINE' on its label, dropped the bottle and grabbed her son. I, of course, was not present during any part of this episode and so I can only draw my own conclusions as to what followed. I will say that, when I arrived home, the air was electric. Marta had her hair wrapped in a towel (she had decided to wash it that afternoon, I was told), there was still a lot of white paint between the tiles on the kitchen walls and floor but, strangest of all, I could only find the now-empty tin of Dulux which I was sure had been ¾ full when I had put it away. This mystery was not solved when I inspected the chair, beautifully painted but it was only a small chair. Not even the sight of our small lawn, now a brilliant white, gave me any clue as to the whereabouts of all the tin's contents. I wasn't really worried about the paint but what did cause me some concern was the language Sylvia may have used (I say 'may have' I should say 'undoubtedly would have' used). After giving this worry some thought, I realised that, unless our au pair had been in a Bilbao dockside bar in the company of some 'scouse' drunken sailors, the words would be alien to her. All Sylvia would say to me was,

"Either she goes or I go," over and over again.

"Now don't be hasty and do anything we'll all be sorry about," I said, doing my best to console her.

"You've not heard it all yet. Not by any means," she spluttered. "Mary Earnshaw came in the shop and I told her. She says if we don't let her look after Jamie from now on like before, she would 'do for' Marta herself and have a contract out on us before the weekend."

"Now that's silly talk. I bet she's been to see 'The Godfather' at the cinema."

"All I know is that she went home saying she was going for an axe."

"In that case, knowing you women and your motherly instincts, give her a ring and ask her to collect him in the morning."

And so, the following morning, Mary arrived (without axe) and it was back to square one. We were very careful not to show any ill feeling towards Marta as she now assumed the position of an average au pair, which was as it should be. She received a number of 'phone calls which she informed us were from her 'boyfriend'. The first three calls originated from Spain but Marta told us that the boy was soon to attend one of London's university colleges and, when he arrived, the number of calls to Marta increased. With Jamie once more in capable hands, life with the Worthingtons became calmer, that is on the five days in seven when Jamie and I were absent from the household. The weekends, however, proved to be just as traumatic.

In the afternoon of the very next Saturday, Marta was in charge of our son. She gathered

the boy, a large amount of his toys and disappeared upstairs after informing Sylvia that she was going to spend the afternoon writing letters 'home' but would attend to Jamie as well. Sylvia passed the message to me.

"Marta is writing letters today. I had hoped she would have done just a little housework whilst you were here to look after Jamie."

"Well why didn't you ask her then?" I asked.

"Oh it doesn't really matter, I'll do it when the shop's closed," she said adding, as she walked back towards the shop, "that is unless you do it now."

"Now just a minute, I'm not watching this cricket on the 'box' for fun, you know."

Sylvia didn't press the point and went back to her customers. I turned my attention back to Trent Bridge but my pleasure had been reduced. After some thought, I stood up and went to my wife.

"It looks to me as if the au pair has taken over control of our lives, but this is the last straw. I will do the housework and, at the same time, undertake the instruction of our au pair. Leave it all to me."

"Go back to the television. I'll do the work tonight."

"No, it's not fair. I'll listen to the Test Match on Radio 3. It's not as good as seeing it but, to help you, I'll manage."

The fact that BBC1 had just left Trent Bridge to visit Cheltenham did not influence my actions so I didn't feel it necessary to mention it to my wife. I quickly began my self-imposed task. I had to hurry as BBC1 returned to cricket in 55 minutes. I washed dishes, vacuumed carpets, dusted and polished furniture and I even mopped the kitchen floor (the Dulux had all but gone). In fact, in three quarters of an hour I had the house shining like a new pin and still had 10 minutes to give Marta her lesson in the thoroughness of English housework.

I climbed the stairs to collect Marta and her ward. I found Marta in her room, as expected, writing her letter. Jamie, I found in another room, happily playing with his toys and his excreta. I picked him up at arm's length, took him to the bathroom, filled the bath and placed him fully-dressed into the water. (He was not as heavy and more willing than a dog, so it wasn't necessary to join him in the water.) Marta appeared at the door of the bathroom and attempted to take over the unpleasant task I had started. I fixed her with an icy stare.

"Down," I grunted, pointing to the stairs. I sounded as if I were talking to a dog. She started to argue so I repeated my command, "Down...today...down."

She understood and went down. I completed the cleaning and returned my son to his more normal sweet-smelling condition. I was not in a very sweet temper when I descended the stairs to carry out the education of an au pair. I found Marta in the shop with Sylvia. They were happily, laughingly discussing my troubles upstairs. They gave the impression of being life-long friends so I took Marta by the arm, saying,

"Come with me," and led her from the shop.

Sylvia followed as I took our au pair on a conducted tour of the house with full attention paid to my earlier work. I mimed dusting, polishing and all the other tasks I had performed and, on completion, I put on my sternest look and in my pleasantest voice said,

"Today, Bob au pair," pointing at myself. "Tomorrow, Marta au pair."

That will have got across, I thought. So, smiling at them, I took my son to continue his education in the intricacies of Derek Underwood's 'wrong run'. I waited through the following week to see the results of Marta's education. I prepared myself for a conducted tour of the house when, on the Saturday afternoon, Marta came to me and, with her sweetest smile, enquired,

"Are you cleaning again today, Measter Worthinkton?"

"No, not today Marta."

(I am even more sure on relating these occurrences that some relative of our au pair visited England's shores and took up employment with Basil Fawlty in his hotel.)

The only other comment I made on the subject that day was to Sylvia. "Either she goes or I go."

Fortunately, Sylvia was not forced to make her choice because, on the Thursday of the next week (after she had received a letter and two 'phone calls), Marta informed us that she was leaving us to join her boyfriend in London. Immediately prior to leaving, she presented us with a Spanish quotation. The translation was along the lines of 'No matter in which house I dwell, my heart will be in yours'. We were all suitably touched but I could not help but feel that we were given the best of the bargain.

cHApTEr 13

During the following 12 months, with my help in gaining a Friday balance, Sylvia grew increasingly proficient in her duties as sub-postmistress. The only other assistance I gave to her in our business venture was in the keeping of the accounts for the Village Store. My growing physical difficulties caused me much embarrassment in carrying out the daily routine of my employment as a Sales Representative. I began to give much thought to the possibility of total self-employment — but what as? That first week when I played the part of 'grocer Bob' had convinced me that, in spite of my family background, I was not cut out to spend my working life behind a counter. I enjoyed selling but not selling over a counter. What I wanted was the cut and thrust of the big wide world on the other side of the hill.

In our last months in suburbia I had formed a partnership with two friends and we had formally registered a company. One of my friends was employed as a Sales Engineer by a national instrument manufacturer, the other was a Draughtsman contracted to one of the country's largest industries. I investigated the chances of expanding this company to the point where it could support me. The task of expanding the Company, in theory at least, I thought should not prove difficult as, during the first 18 months of its existence, its turnover was running (creeping) at £50 (that is not £50 a week or even month, just a turnover of £50).

The difficult bit, I was sure, would be in supporting me. Once more, the answer to this problem, like so many others, appeared with a little help from my friends.

I was introduced to the Managing Director of a London-based company which manufactured accessories for our company with a certain type of electronic recording instrument. He offered me the opportunity of selling the company's products on a straight commission exclusively in the North of England. After discussion with my wife ("whatever you wish"), consulting with my partners ("It's your neck"), asking Glenys and Les ("be sure you don't make a mistake") and considering Mother (I daren't tell her), I decided to give it a whirl.

I took a week's holiday and, in the car we had bought for Sylvia (to use on her trips to the warehouse), I made visits to a number of prospective customers' works and offices. The amount of orders and promises of orders I received during these few days convinced me that the offer I had received from London was, indeed, the answer to my problems. I therefore made another flying visit (this time without any desire to sky dive) to inform my employers of my intention and I gave notice of resignation. My news was accepted graciously with a promise that any order I could obtain for their products during the course of my future independent travels would gain a 10% commission for me.

The start of this second venture within two years into the world of commerce was delayed for a further three months, being the period required to terminate my contract of employment. This time, during which I received monthly cheques, was spent in preparing the way to a secure future. I didn't totally neglect the business of the company who furnished those three cheques, but perhaps, despite the assurance at the close of all my letters to every customer, 'my best attentions' were focussed on my own new company's future affairs. I found that during the many 'calls' I made in this period and, in fact from this time forth, my whole approach was very different when representing my own company to that when I was representing my previous employer. No doubt any psychiatrist could explain these changes in my feelings and actions. All I know is that as I hobbled (with my ever present walking stick) about the industrial and teaching establishments I visited, depending on which 'hat' I was wearing, I would change from a 'poor cripple' to a slightly disabled entrepreneur. (These feelings persisted even when visiting customers I had visited many times in years past.)

The order level resulting from my visits indicated that my new and old customers saw me in a different light as well. The turnover of £50 did increase to the target point where it could and did support me in the manner to which I had become accustomed prior to 'going it alone'. I discovered, in the first weeks of self-employment, that there was a 'band' of representatives who, for various reasons, had travelled similar roads to mine and they assisted each other in many ways. I obtained more agency agreements and then began to manufacture simple special 'one off' pieces of electronic equipment, progressing to more complex equipment in fairly large quantities. This development of my company took place over a number of years and I took no part in the actual manufacture of the equipment. My hands trembled, making my efforts with a soldering iron dangerous in execution and useless on completion.

Whether my rushing up and down the countryside at this time retarded or accelerated my disease, no-one has said but, during those first couple of years of active self-employment I was more successful in my chosen career than at any time before. It gave me a taste of what could have been. The number of times I've said (and the number of people I've bored), "If only I'd been born healthy instead of handsome," or, "I feel as if I've graduated from university but MS has prevented me from practising."

I was always very conscious of my lack of stability but continued to try to disguise my very obvious disabilities — although I depended on a walking stick to make any progress in an upright position. In retrospect, I am sure I only succeeded in accentuating my disability. However, on one or two occasions, I did 'lay it on a bit' and, to my satisfaction, found that, should the mood take me, I could make more physically able people show a little respect to us 'cripples'.

One of these occasions occurred during a visit to a section of one of the nation's nationalised industries. These establishments are staffed, in the main, by intelligent, well-educated personnel who know their particular field intimately and are interested only in the specification and performance of any equipment they purchase. (In many cases it is almost as if it is their money they are being asked to spend, not ours!)

However, this area of the market invariably has, hidden amongst its staff, at least one person who believes himself to be in all matters superior and insists, continually, on proving it — or at least endeavouring to prove it (mainly to himself). In matters technical, the opportunities to put such a person's knowledge to the test are very rare and, on the odd occasion I tried, it was always my face the egg landed on. It was one of these characters, whose name I had been given as a contact, I visited on this day.

I presented myself at the reception desk and gave my name and that of my contact to a pretty young lady receptionist. Using her telephone, she contacted the man I wished to see. After speaking to him for a few moments, she turned back to me.

"He says he will be out to see you as soon as he is able. If you will wait over there you should see him coming up the passage in a minute or two," she said, indicating the entrance to a long corridor that led to the offices and laboratories making up the main working areas of the building.

I turned and slowly walked towards the mouth of the passage after giving her a smile of thanks.

"Would you like a chair, Mr Worthington?" she called after me, on watching how my walking stick aided my still-unsteady movement.

"No thank you," I answered. "I prefer to stand – I sit down too much in the car."

"What a lovely girl," I thought. "I bet she thinks I'm a fighter pilot who's had a nasty prang or maybe a racing driver involved in a shunt. I remained standing as motionless as MS permitted for 10 minutes or so, during which time the passage remained completely deserted. I studied the attractive female as she continued with the work which receptionists have to do when not attending to visitors. Possibly she became aware of my approving looks because she suddenly lifted her head from the papers on her desk.

"Would you like me to give him another ring?" she enquired with a sweet smile.

"Don't worry," I replied very quickly, my thoughts still in the clouds. "So long as I get to Oulton Park in time for the first race this afternoon, I've lots of time."

"I didn't know there was any racing at Oulton today," she said as my mind 'blew'. "My husband drives for the Cheshire Club and he never mentioned anything."

"Oh well," was all I managed before she continued.

"If you go there often you more than likely know him. His name is (she named him) — he drives a Lotus Elan."

Isn't it funny how pretty girls lose all their charm as soon as they speak — at least this one did.

"Did I say Oulton Park? I meant to say Trafford Park," I spluttered and was saved from explaining what was to race on Manchester's large industrial estate that afternoon when I saw a movement at the far end of the passage.

A man appeared through the furthermost door, took a step towards me but stopped on seeing me swaying at the other end and shouted, "If you wanna see me, better use your legs – they are younger than mine."

During my wait for this character, I had been viewing the long corridor with apprehension but now, when I had to move down its length, (in spite of my hurry to escape from the embarrassing conversation with Mrs Stewart) I decided to use my disability to its full. When I followed my contact's instruction to use my young legs, the movements I made gave me the appearance of a 90-year-old arthritic with stones in his shoes. My actions had the desired effect.

Before I had progressed a yard, my contact was running up the passage calling, "It's OK. I'm sorry. Stay there. I'll come to you."

The receptionist glided across the foyer, reaching me seconds earlier than the running man.

"I did ask if you wanted to sit down," she complained.

My contact arrived and I allowed them to help me sit down. I gave my thanks to the young lady and graciously accepted the order that was forced on to me by the older man of a cup of tea that appeared as if by magic.

Not many orders were gained by this subterfuge but, as I had supplied similar equipment to this customer's counterpart in other areas of the industry to their satisfaction, my conscience was clear.

All the profits that my efforts produced were spent in converting the two-storey building at the side of the post office into an office and workshop. I employed a young woman who efficiently took care of the necessary paperwork and accounts involved in agency selling. This healthy state was not to last as MS made further inroads into my myelin sheaths (sorry). It was only a matter of months before I was unable to carry out my visits to customers' premises to endeavour (by fair means or foul) to obtain orders. But, wiping the tears from my eyes, I will continue with my tale.

cHApTEr 14

We received the first of our two visits from the criminal classes around half past eight in the evening of a late autumn day. After seeing the children safely into bed, Sylvia and I were stealing an hour from our business duties to watch the exploits of Charlie Barlow and John Watt[8], with no realisation that we were shortly to be involved with a similar body of men to those we were watching actors portray on the television.

I left Sylvia safely in the hands of the Regional Crime Squad and, having switched on the lights, I went into the shop to collect the day's takings.

I had just got my hands into the till when there was a knocking on the door of the shop. Ensuring that my body screened the till and its contents, I looked over my shoulder towards the door. Through one of the two diamond-shaped windows in the door I could see a stranger's face but, before its owner had time to speak, I shouted, "Sorry, but we're closed."

As the face disappeared into the darkness outside, I smuggled the money from the till into the front of my shirt and, with a sideways movement, keeping my back to the door, I re-joined my wife and the television policemen.

---

8 TV Series at the time called 'Softly Softly Task Force'.

I deposited the money into my armchair and, after telling Sylvia, "We've got strangers on the car park. You count that money. I'm going to see what they are up to."

I returned to the now-darkened shop. I crept fumblingly through the shop to the front window from where I looked down the car park to the 'phone box, which stood some 30 yards away. I crouched on the floor and peered along the bottom of the window display area and saw, through the pyramid displays of tins and packets, the illuminated kiosk. In this light I could see three young chaps. One was on hands and knees inside, a second was standing in the doorway of the telephone box, holding open the heavily sprung door and the third member of the group was standing at the periphery of the small circle of light which spread out of the kiosk.

I prepared to analyse the situation by observations. My cover was excellent. In the gloomy blackness of the shop the subjects of my observations stood no chance of seeing me between tins of fruit and packets of soap powder. That is until Sylvia, who had crept silently through the darkness so as not to miss the action, laid her hands on my shoulders. With a sharp intake of breath, I collapsed backwards with shock but not before my arms had shot forward, searching for a firm handhold, only to find the bottom row of a pyramid of tins. Sylvia stepped back to allow my fall to progress unhindered which ended with me in company with, what seemed at the time, dozens of cans of all varieties of fruit.

"What are they doing?" she whispered.

"Sod them!" I wept. "What the hell are you doing? If they chose to demolish the whole property, they couldn't do more harm than you've just done to my nervous system."

"Sorry," was all the apology she offered.

"For God's sake, don't creep about like that," I muttered as I struggled back to a more upright stance.

"Oh look!" said Sylvia, apparently still unaware of my pounding heart. "They are still there. They mustn't have heard you make all that noise."

"Me? Me make all the noise? It's like being married to Dracula's daughter. Just help me to a chair. When my heartbeat returns to something approaching normal I may, and I promise nothing, turn my attention to the protection of 'your' 'phone box."

I allowed Sylvia to help me from my hiding place, kicking whatever of the scattered window display came into contact with my feet. I regained my composure after sitting in an armchair in front of the television for a few minutes.

"I'm OK now," I said to Sylvia. "Switch on all the lights in the front of the house. If they're up to no good, that will frighten them away."

She did as requested and illuminated the front of the whole property as I climbed the stairs to a better vantage of the scene outside. The extra light that we had given to the area in which we were interested had not deterred our visitors. The two suspected thieves in the kiosk were not making a telephone call. In fact, they appeared to be dismantling the complete range of equipment contained in the small cubicle.

I let the curtain fall slowly back into place and, equally slowly, descended the stairs to re-join my wife.

"I'm going out to them," I announced, sounding far braver than I felt (but then had I not just seen Inspector Hawkins tackle a gang of armed gangsters single-handed?). "You get ready by our 'phone and, if there is the slightest sign of trouble, ring the police."

With the feeling of déjà vu, collecting my walking stick purely to use as an aid to walking but with a hope that the villains outside would see it as an invincible weapon, I unlocked the shop door and stepped out into the cold night. I advanced about 10 paces in my unsteady gait before I was noticed. The two villains in the 'phone box stopped their nefarious work and looked in my direction.

"What are you doing?" I called in my sternest voice.

There was no answer to my question but a cry came from the darkness away to my left.

"Run!"

I heard that there is no honour amongst thieves and what happened in the following few seconds proved that statement to be true. The person who had shouted "Run", no doubt a lookout man, would be in full flight by now. The chap who was holding the door ajar deserted his post at speed, leaving the door to slowly but powerfully swing closed as the remaining member of the trio, trying to rise from his kneeling position, fell through the decreasing space between door and doorway. The door spring did not have sufficient strength to hold him but it did serve to increase his panic. If I had had the inclination and the ability to even walk (instead of stagger) I would have had ample time to 'feel his collar'. However, at that cry of "Run", I put my every effort into following the instruction but in the opposite direction to that taken by the criminals.

By the time I had reached the security of the shop, Sylvia was on the telephone with the local constabulary and they informed her that there was a patrol car in our vicinity which they would direct to us. Within a few minutes, a 'Panda' drove onto our car park but, unfortunately, in those few minutes, the three villains would have had ample time to disappear into the surrounding countryside. The policeman who emerged from the car obviously realised this as he offered no chase. Instead, he joined us in the shop and listened to the main points of our observations. Not wanting to have my wife arrested for conspiracy, I did not inform on her almost successful attempt to blow my cover by frightening the life out of me during the course of my investigations. Then he strode over to the kiosk with Sylvia and I close behind.

Our three visitors, if nothing else, certainly knew how to dismantle the equipment installed in a telephone call box. The complete mechanism had been removed from the wall of the kiosk, leaving only a piece of wood and a number of wires hanging from it to show its original position. The telephone, with all its mountings including the money container, stood on the floor of the kiosk. The officer of the law inspected the vandalised equipment and decided to take the entire evidence down to the local police station.

On hearing his intentions, Sylvia, who up to this point had remained silent, spoke, "You can't do that," she said. "At least not yet. I am the sub-postmistress of this village and, before I can allow you to take this piece of GPO property, I have certain duties to perform.' With this she ran back into the shop, calling over her shoulder, "Wait there. I'll only be a minute."

She reappeared from the shop within a few minutes to re-join her mystified but proud husband and the policeman. As she walked back towards us, it would have been impossible not to have noticed a large piece of cardboard, at least two feet square, which she carried banner-like in front of herself. Sellotaped to one side of this cardboard was a printed notice. She spoke again.

"Whenever the 'phone is out of order, I have been instructed to put up this notice."

Without further words, she very carefully hung her notice from the disconnected wires attached to a piece of wood which previously held the equipment that was the reason for this little red building's existence.

Sylvia stood back, holding open the door. She adjusted the sign until it met with her full professional approval and then, with a satisfied look of duty fulfilled, she turned to the constable, "That's OK now, you can take the 'phone."

The policeman and I looked at Sylvia's handiwork and then looked at each other. The policeman smiled and, quickly loading the telephone into his car, he drove off our car park.

As he passed us he was smiling broadly and we both heard him say to no-one in particular, "Wait till I tell them this at the station."

As the police car disappeared down the dark village road, Sylvia turned to find me still smiling.

"What's wrong with him?" she asked.

"Just have another look at your notice," I suggested. "If some poor unfortunate foreigner finds himself stranded in these parts and, on finding this kiosk he should fail to notice the absence of the usual necessary equipment, well then your notice would be invaluable."

The notice, you see, read explicitly 'THIS TELEPHONE IS OUT OF ORDER' in English, French, German, Spanish, Italian and three other languages which I have never seen, either before or since. On reflection, the only language missing was the one that would have been needed, all things taken into consideration: Braille.

We heard a few days later that 3 boys who had absconded from a nearby remand home, on being caught, had admitted to doing a number of call boxes, one of which was ours.

My disability had a couple of years to worsen before we received our second visit from the criminal fraternity. One Sunday night we had retired to bed soon after midnight and, a few minutes after switching out the light, we heard the sound of a car door being closed outside on the car park. This noise was not uncommon but was normally preceded by the sounds of a car being driven up to the 'phone box. Neither Sylvia nor I spoke but lay waiting for further noises. We heard whispering voices which was in itself unusual as, even with the bedroom window closed, we had heard one side of many an interesting telephone conversation quite audibly. After lying and listening for a few minutes, we both arose in unison from our individual side of the bed and went to the bedroom window.

Slowly we moved the curtains and looked out to see a small car parked to the side of the kiosk. Inside the call box were two men who, we could clearly see from our elevated position, were in no way making a telephone call. In fact, one of the men had a large hammer and he was preparing to smash his way into the money container. Without doubt, I thought, the intelligence of the crooks in our area was definitely on a downward slope. Possibly this gang had arrived at a more suitable time for their type of work; they had driven up to the scene of the intended crime, waited quietly in their car until the last light had been extinguished in the nearby property and then got out, slammed the car door, and attacked their target with a 10-pound sledgehammer. On hearing the first sounds of hammer on telephone, we leapt into action. I say we leapt into action, in actual fact Sylvia did the leaping. I assumed the well-earned role of Commander-in-Chief, albeit a disabled one. (They didn't strip John Wayne of his stars when he was injured during 'The Longest Day'.)

"Downstairs! Get the number of the car first and then ring the police," I ordered.

Sylvia departed at the double to carry out my orders so I turned my attention back to watching the demolition of the kiosk's contents. My first lieutenant returned after a few minutes to report mission completed so we both settled down at the window to await the arrival of the Flying Squad and, we hoped, the ensuing gun battle (television has a lot to answer for). On that night the police did not arrive until a minute after the criminals, defeated by the Post Office's latest re-enforced public telephone equipment, drove away from the battered but triumphant kiosk. On first sight of the car with its blue light flashing, I dispersed my available troop.

"Quick! Downstairs! Give the police the car number and tell them the crooks have just gone off over the canal bridge," I instructed as if Sylvia had not witness exactly the same as I.

She jumped from the sitting position we had both adopted to get a comfortable view of the action below and rushed to greet the constabulary who had jumped from their car, raced to the shop door and now appeared to be trying to smash it down. I watched my wife open the door and, in a brief conversation, I heard her give the two policemen instructions. Then they ran back to the car and disappeared, at high speed, in pursuit of the disappointed criminals.

Sylvia was soon sitting at my side and we remained on watch for a further 30 minutes. Nothing more happened during this time except for the passing of a different police car but, as its occupants didn't choose to stop to give us a progress report of the chase, we became bored and went back to bed.

The next morning, I rang the police station and was given the full details of the previous night's chase which had culminated in the arrest of the 'hammer swinger' and his accomplice.

Over the following days, we received a number of visits from the police during which we were asked to make statements, the 'everything you say will be taken down and may be used in evidence' type of statement. They were used in evidence. We saw our names in the newspaper reports of the court proceedings. They made us appear to be very brave and public spirited and made no mention of the fact that at no time did we leave the safety and comfort of our bedroom. It must have been these reports which the Post Office authorities read as, a couple of weeks later, the sub-postmistress received a letter from the Postmaster General congratulating her on her actions. This was pleasant but, more important than the letter, was the cheque for £10 which was stapled to it.

cHApTEr 15

It must have been six to eight months after that first visit of the kiosk criminals when, as I was still able to drive and walk short distances, I decided to follow up a tip I had received from a friend who represented my previous employers. I arranged to visit, in the company of my friend, one of his customers who had a requirement for a large quantity of a certain type of instrument for which I had an agency agreement. The fact that this customer's office was situated in the far north of my area caused me no concern. I made a mental check of all the private and public conveniences on my intended route and, making an early start, I drove to Durham. I spent a pleasant, busy and successful day with my friend and his customers and eventually took leave of them and started the journey home.

I drove on to the car park at around 11 o'clock on a cold, wet night, more than a little tired and very hungry. Sylvia appeared at the side door to welcome me and, before I had time to open the lean-to garage doors, Sasha, the Labrador dog that had taken Kim's position (now two years old or more and much larger) bounded out from behind her to add his own additional welcome to the master.

"Do you want something to eat or have you been 'living it up' on the way?" Sylvia called as I struggled with the dog who impeded all my efforts to open the garage doors.

"I've not eaten since lunch-time," I answered truthfully, giving the dog a friendly kick in the ribs.

"Fetch!" I shouted to him, throwing an imaginary stone towards the rough piece of ground between the car park and the canal. Sasha disappeared into the darkness with loud barking and I turned my attention back to my wife who remained in the shelter of the house.

"I'll settle for a fry-up," I called. "I'm too weary and hungry to wait for anything else."

Sylvia retreated into the house to prepare the food of my choice and, without the dog's assistance, I put the car into the garage. I could hear Sasha searching for the non-existent stone so I called to him. When he did not come in answer and, as it was still raining and realising his feet would be wet and muddy, I decided to let him have half an hour's play whilst I ate my food.

I went indoors and sat in front of a roaring fire, getting warm and dry. I could hear Sylvia and the lovely sound of her frying pan doing its work on my bacon and eggs. I ate my supper from a plate on my knees. This was the manner of eating all our meals, with the exception of breakfast, since our arrival at the village store. Sylvia drank a cup of tea as she watched me devouring the 'fry-up' and we exchanged our individual day's news. It had been a good day in the shop and I told Sylvia of the orders I had been promised so, in a contented frame of mind, we decided it was time for sleeping. I remembered that Sasha was still out-of-doors so, as Sylvia went upstairs, I went to the side door and, looking out into the cold, wet night I called his name a number of times. There was neither sight nor sound of him. I shut and locked the door and climbed the stairs to join my wife.

"He's not for coming in, blast him!" I complained to her. "I've locked him out and it serves him right."

"Oh, you can't do that," she said, "not on a night like this."

"Just watch me!" I snapped, too tired to enter into an argument about the dog.

"But Bob, a boat went through the lock just as it was going dark. They've probably moored for the night just further up the canal towpath and, if they are kept awake all night by a barking dog, they are not likely to come to the shop in the morning unless it's to complain."

"Look love, I'm absolutely shattered. If he starts barking I will get up and let him in," I said, believing that, as soon as we were asleep, roaring lions would not waken us – or so I thought!

Only a few minutes later, in a nice warm bed, we bid each other goodnight and turned out the light. The bread man would arrive in a few short hours.

I was not very sure what the noise was when first I heard it or even if I heard anything at all. It was so quiet — but then it came again.

"Can you hear the dog crying?" asked Sylvia, who not only had heard the sound but had recognised it.

"Hear what, my dear?" I answered her, hoping that we would hear no more. But, as I spoke, the noise came again.

"There it is again; didn't you hear it?" she pressed.

"Yes, my beloved, I can hear it. It's your dog crying to come in. You'd better get up and let him in," I said, chancing my arm.

"Oh, come on now. You said that if he barked you'd get up and see to him."

"Yes – but I've not heard him bark yet." (No flies on me!)

"It's my turn to see to the bread man in the morning. You're always saying he's your dog so come on, get up and let him in."

I had to admit that it was her turn for the bread man, the most disliked job in our life, so shared day in, day out. I got out of bed, put on my dressing gown and, with an exaggerated disabled stagger, I left the bedroom, went down the stairs and through the house to the side door. I opened the door and called into the cold night air.

"Come on, boy!"

But Sasha did not come in answer. I called again, listening after each call, expecting to at least hear him bark on recognising my voice. I could hear no sound of barking, only an occasional whimper and that only just audible. I ventured through the door onto the car park. It had ceased raining but, dressed in pyjamas and dressing gown, the cold and damp night was anything but welcoming. I stopped to consider a course of action that would lead to my earliest return to a well-earned warm bed and sleep. Suddenly I remembered that the last time I had seen the dog was just as I was putting the car into the garage. A chill ran through me as I quickly considered the possibility of having run him down inside the garage with the poor, wounded animal still trapped under the car wheels. As these thoughts were running through my mind, I staggered back into the house to collect the bunch of keys, including those of garage and car. I opened the garage doors with foreboding and almost collapsed with relief on finding he was not there. I listened again and now I could hear his cries much clearer. During the last five to ten minutes, my normally limited energies had been rapidly diminishing. There was little choice but to summon up my ever-present and ever-worked troop so, returning indoors, I called up the staircase.

"Come and help me look for him. I can hear him quite plainly but he's nowhere to be seen."

Sylvia joined me very quickly and we both went outside to the car park.

"You have a look in the lock," I instructed. "I'll see if he had fallen into the weir."

The weir was at the side of the garage. Its purpose was to allow water to bypass the lock during rainy weather (similar to the weather on that particular night) when lack of canal traffic through the lock led to the level on the upstream side rising above the acceptable.

We rushed in different directions; both of us, by this time, very anxious to know the whereabouts of the family pet. I leaned over the wall that guarded the weir, peered into the dark torrent of water that was disappearing through a metal grille, the object of which was to stop any foreign bodies being plunged into the overflow pipe that carried the excess water underground, releasing it downstream from the lock. As I strained to see if our dog was pinned against the grille, Sylvia's voice came through the darkness.

"Quick, Bob! He's fallen in the lock," she shouted and, to add to the sinking feeling in my stomach, she continued, "and the lock's empty."

The lock at the side of our property dropped the canal twelve feet, so meaning that the dog had had a nasty fall into three feet of cold, dirty water that remained when the lock was empty. I moved at my highest speed across the rough ground to where Sylvia was looking into the black cavern of the empty lock. I peered down into the inky blackness and guessed the location of the animal purely by the whimpering sounds he was still making.

"Help me to open the gates," I shouted as I moved towards and then began to push against the wooden beam that would open the massive gates at the mouth of the lock. Sylvia quickly added her weight to mine and we both strained with every muscle but the gates refused to open. I knew the reason for our lack of success. British Waterways canals are in a very poor state of repair. This is understandable as most of them are between 150 and 200 years old and, as the traffic on the canals is at present 99% pleasure craft, there is little money to bring the waterways into the twentieth century. The lock that this night contained Sasha was no exception. Over a relatively short period, enough water would leak through the lock's top gates to cause the water in the lock to rise, perhaps only one or two inches, but sufficient to hold the bottom gates firmly closed.

To release this pressure of water is very simple if you possess a 'windlass'. The windlass is an essential piece of equipment for all canal users as it is used to raise and lower the paddles found at each end of every lock thereby flooding or draining the lock as required. Of course, we had no windlass.

"What can we do?" Sylvia cried, very close to tears. "Sasha's going to drown."

I could hear more than see that she was right. In all probability, the dog had been in the water for more than an hour. This, together with his fall and the energy he must have used in struggling to climb the vertical walls surrounding him, would have brought the time when he goes to the forest in the sky very near.

I looked along the canal and, through the gloom, I could just make out the shape of a pleasure boat in complete darkness; it was moored at the towpath side of the canal about 100 yards from the lock. We were to learn the following morning that there were two young couples aboard, having an early season holiday on the canals. They had retired to bed around the time I had arrived home from Durham and were now in a deep sleep after a very hard day working up the dozens of locks along our stretch of the Trent and Mersey Canal.

"Run up and borrow their windlass," I said to Sylvia, pointing to the boat she had seen passing through the lock that evening.

She did not have to be asked twice as, by this time, she was in an advanced state of panic. She went like a bullet from a gun, up the towpath, shouting loudly as she went. "Help, help, can we have your windlass?"

She arrived at the silent boat and commenced to hammer with both her firsts on its roof. "Quick, quick, wake up, damn you! I want your windlass – our dog's drowning."

Now, if the people in the boat had been professional 'boaters' they would doubtless have weighed up the situation within a second and given my now-hysterical wife what she requested. However, this boat receiving my wife's undivided attentions held four sleep-drugged city dwellers who were unprepared for a crazy woman arriving in the dead of night, beating a tattoo on the roof, only inches above their heads, screaming for an unknown something called a windlass. Within fractions of a second there were equally loud screams emitting from inside the boat as four bodies fell, jumped and fought to escape from the very real nightmare that continued drumming just above their heads, demanding the windlass.

"There's a woman outside who wants a windlass," came a girl's voice, obviously fighting a losing battle to keep control of her jangled nerves.

"Well, for God's sake, give her one," came back a man's voice.

"I only wish I could," said the first voice.

"I'll give her one," shouted a second man's voice. "If only somebody would tell me what the hell a windlass is."

"I know, I know," shouted the last member of the crew. "But I don't know where it is. You had it last, Brian – it's that spanner thing you use on the locks."

They began a noisy search but it took minutes before the windlass was located and given to Sylvia.

Meanwhile, on hearing all the shouting and screaming coming out of the gloom, I tried once more and applied all my strength to the beam. In this desperate moment I must have found a little extra strength because the lock gate moved. The movement was only the merest fraction but it was sufficient to allow the water that caused the pressure to flow through the gap I had made. It was now easier to move it until the gap increased to about 18" but, then, with every ounce of my strength spent, I was unable to move it any more. I was struggling and straining and just managing to prevent the gates from swinging back to their original position. I called to the dog, pleading for him to swim through the gap and out of the lock. I could not see him and was afraid that, if I released the gates, he would be crushed by the great weight of them closing. Nonetheless, I could not hold them open any longer. I collapsed over the beam but the pain in my back abated when I heard Sasha, still whimpering, on the canal side of the lock. Sylvia arrived at this jubilant moment with the windlass.

"Take the bloody thing back!" I gasped. "The dog's free."

Poor Sylvia was breathless but, without a word of complaint, she about-faced and ran back up the towpath until when, about 10 yards from the boat, she tossed the windlass high in the air in the direction of the slowly settling vessel.

"Thanks, but we've managed," she shouted, turning back to join me, as the shouting and screaming started again from the nerve-shattered holidaymakers when Sylvia's aim proved true and their windlass landed with a resounding crash on the roof of their boat.

I had picked myself up very wearily, but only to a kneeling crouch. I crawled in this position across a small footbridge to the towpath side of the 'cut' and, still on hands and knees, went along the muddy ground, down the slope that brought me to canal level. Sasha had followed my slow progress, swimming alongside me. I reached a less uneven piece of canal bank; the dog swam to where I lay but was too exhausted to climb from the water so, finding what had to be my very last drop of muscle, I gripped a handful of skin and hair at the back of the dog's neck and dragged him to my side. He struggled up until he stood on his four legs, bent his head to lick my face and then, as all animals do on coming out of the water, shook himself vigorously. When he had finished this natural function, the only way it was possible to tell which had been in the canal – man or dog – was that the man was covered in mud.

Sylvia was very pleased that the blasted dog had been rescued and she carried the dear animal indoors with many 'Ooh's' and 'Aah's'. She then returned to pick me up from the towpath where I still lay and carried me into the house. The dog and I sat side by side in front of the dying fire as Sylvia bathed Sasha's blood-covered paws. The damage to his paws, we assumed, had been done in his efforts to scale the lock walls. I was soaked to the skin, my pyjamas were covered in mud and, on inspection, we discovered that the blood was not all Sasha's, some of it was mine. There was a neat slit in what little flesh was left on my knee. As the medics would say, it was laid bare to my patella. My knee received a quick dab of Dettol after I had a hot bath and dressed in dry clothes. As Sylvia had already bedded down our pet, I was helped into bed. Sylvia joined me and, in no time at all, the bread man arrived.

cHAptEr 16

When the bread man arrived on the following morning, Sylvia did take her turn and attend to him. The fact that it was her turn was immaterial. Should it have been my turn, I found, on trying to raise myself from a lying position that, if not impossible, then it was extremely painful. My efforts in rescuing Sasha from the empty lock had taken their toll. I was sure that my back was broken in at least four places!

Sylvia returned to our bedroom after collecting the amount of bread she would require to satisfy her customers' daily needs. "Are you all right?" she asked me on hearing my moans and obvious difficulties in moving.

"Apart from a few fractures in my spine and an ache in every muscle in my body, I'm as right as a four penny piece," I croaked.

"I think you ought to stay where you are for the day," she said, very concerned.

"I can't stay here. I've got a couple of calls to make and I want to take that panel into the university to be given its final tests. It has to be delivered before the weekend."

"Well at least let me make an appointment for you to see the doctor," my caring wife suggested.

"Please don't worry, pet. Seriously, I'm OK," I assured her. "If you'll just help me out of this blasted bed, I'll be fine."

Sylvia did as I requested and I found that when I was upright, apart from a pain in my lower back, I was able to walk in the usual unsteady stagger. We both dressed and, after Sylvia had seen our daughter off to the village school and our son into Mary's capable hands, she opened the shop and I drove away to try to persuade some customer to sign one of his order forms.

The day passed without any traumas. I found that the pain in my back lessened as the day progressed. I had discovered many moons ago that, at this stage of my affair with MS, it never impeded my ability to control my car. I would stagger and stumble until I was sitting behind the steering wheel when 15 years of driving experience, covering many thousands of miles in all types of weather, would come to my rescue. I must add that the help this experience gave to me did not last for long after I took to rescuing animals in the cold, wet midnight hours.

Sylvia was very pleased when I arrived home on that evening.

"How have you been today, Lover?" was the question she greeted me with.

"As soon as I was mobile my back gave me no trouble at all," I informed her.

"Well I still think you should see the doctor," she stated before commencing to prepare some food.

"Look my dear, it's Friday tomorrow. If I have any trouble then I'll pop into the doctor's first thing Saturday morning, if that will make you happy."

Why can't a woman be as uncaring as a man.

We didn't have to wait until the 'morrow' before I had trouble with my back. When we prepared for bed I discovered I was unable to manipulate my back, legs and arms in the manner required to leave me horizontal on the bed. After much grunting and groaning, Sylvia (with very little constructive help from me), managed to lower me to the sleeping surface. I had the appearance of a corpse who had been expertly 'laid out'.

"Will you be OK like that?" I was asked by my own lovely helpmate and mortician.

"Yes, I'm very comfortable," I lied as, already, a feeling was spreading through me which led me to believe that, if I didn't move soon, I would set like a jelly.

Sylvia believed me, however, and so she walked round the foot of the bed and climbed in beside me. "Good night," she said. "I will get up for the bread man in the morning."

"Thank you, darling. Goodnight and get a good night's sleep," I said, fighting the increasing feeling of rigidity. I fought a losing battle for 5 minutes before I submitted. "I'm sorry Sylvia but I've got to get up. Will you help me please?"

"Don't worry. You can't help it. I'll go and get a bottle if that will do."

"No, love. I don't want to go to the 'loo'. I just want to stand up.'

My understanding wife threw back the bed covers and once more came to my side of the bed. With a similar struggle and even more grunts and groans than had accompanied my 'laying out', Sylvia succeeded in gaining for me an upright posture.

"Now what do you want to do?" she asked, not unkindly.

"Nothing," I told her. "You get back into bed. I just want to stand here for a few moments and perhaps walk round the bedroom a couple of times and then I'll come back to bed."

"Are you sure you'll be able to manage?" She wasn't at all convinced that, now I was standing on my two feet, I was cured.

"You get back to bed and sleep. I'm 100% OK," I reassured her.

Still very concerned, Sylvia climbed into the bed and, pulling the covers back over her, she curled up and prepared for the Sandman's call. I watched her as I leaned against the bedroom wall opposite. There was no doubt that the pain definitely receded when I was standing. I took a few steps around the space between bed and wall without taking either of my hands from the wall's firm surface. In 10 minutes, I returned to my original position, leaning against the wall closest to my side of the bed. I looked across to Sylvia; by this time she was sound asleep. She had watched my first unsteady movements at the start of my trip around the bedroom walls but must have dropped off during my return journey. First I made a move to sit on the bed. I managed this with only a small amount of pain and difficulty. It was when I attempted to raise my legs from the floor that I was forced to cry out. Whether it was a cry of pain or my words that brought my wife back to the land of the living, I'm not sure.

"Sylvia, I'm very sorry to waken you but would you help me back into bed please?"

"Yes, of course," a sleepy but understanding wife replied and, in total silence apart from my grunts and groans, had me in the corpse-like position I had assumed prior to my 'stroll'. Once more she climbed into bed, wished me goodnight for the second time and, I could tell from the rhythm of her breathing, was asleep in seconds.

I lay in the near darkness and kept my thoughts on any and everything. As long as I didn't think of jellies I would be OK and wouldn't wobble. I concentrated on the work I had planned to carry out with the help of one of my partners the following Saturday morning. Over the last three Saturday and Sunday mornings, we had made good progress in improving the company's office and workshop. Only two days ago I had ordered two cubic yards of ready-mixed concrete for making a better floor. Then my thought control took a bad fall. I went through the schedule of work. I thought 'I wonder how long cement takes to . . .'. I never completed the thought. I had set.

"Sylvia, Sylvia, please wake up. I've got to get up now."

No doubt feeling guilty for the torment she had given the canal holidaymakers only 24 hours earlier, she got up again and I gave a repeat performance of my walking tour. Her guilt and understanding stretched through the next three tours and, as she laid me out for the fourth time, at the end of the 3.00 am performance, she completed her undertaker's act with a firm and far-from-understanding blow to my chest.

"S.L.E.E.P – that's what you need! If you want to get up again do it very, very quietly and do not WAKE ME."

The volume of her orders assisted me in my efforts to make a rapid journey into the land of dreams.

I woke the following morning, still in a corpse-like position but alone in the bed. I looked at my watch to find Sylvia had allowed my sleep to continue undisturbed. It was half past ten. As I lay, slowly testing my ability to move, I could hear our customers below being supplied with their daily bread. To my surprise and relief, I rose from a sleeping position that, for me, was most unusual — with only minor pain when compared to the struggle, grunts and groans of a few hours earlier. I dressed after doing minimum ablutions, went down to the kitchen and was half way through my morning bowl of cornflakes when Sylvia appeared from the shop.

"Why didn't you stay in bed? I don't think you had a very good night."

"I'm sorry if I woke you up but I'm fine now."

"It doesn't matter about that but I think you're silly if you don't go back to bed."

"I told you yesterday, I've got that panel to collect from the university then deliver it to the customer. It's very important that it's delivered to them as promised or we'll never get another order there."

"It won't matter if you get another order or not if you're dead."

"Mum is coming for the weekend," I reminded her. "She won't let me die. I promised you I'd go to the doctors tomorrow and I will."

Sylvia gave me her despairing look and the argument was at an end. My unhappy wife returned to the shop and soon I was on the motorway en route for the university.

I stopped at a wine store on this journey to buy a bottle of sparkling wine. I had promised my friend at the university, who not only was testing the panel I was hoping to collect that day but who had designed the electronic circuitry within and had done most of its construction, that, on completion of this project (the largest single order we had obtained up to date), we would share a bottle of champagne. Company funds would not, however, 'run' to the genuine 'bubbly' so I decided sparkling wine would have to suffice.

Immediately on leaving the M6 to drive through the built-up areas that led to the city centre, I stopped at the first shop I saw which, in my younger days, was called an 'Off door licence' but now was referred to as a 'Winery'. I parked the car close to the pavement and, leaning on my walking stick (more heavily than normally), I entered the 'boozery'. I was shown a selection of bottles containing the type of wine I wanted. I made my choice, based not on quality but purely on price, and lurched back across the flagstones towards my parked car. When I was slightly less than a body's length from the vehicle, the toe of my shoe came into contact with an uneven piece of paving stone. I did my utmost to save myself from a heavy fall but, with a bottle in one hand and a useless walking stick in the other, all my arm-swinging efforts were in vain. In apparent slow motion I saw that section of the car body which in the earlier designs of cars was known as the 'running board'. Unless I took immediate evading action, this would bring the downward movement of my head to an abrupt stop. The first involuntary action my senses took was to eject the bottle from my hands. The bottle shattered on impact with the pavement, showering my body with its contents. Fortunately, my knees hit the ground before the glass so that there was no blood there and my hands hit the car before my head so there was no fractured skull.

I dragged myself up onto my feet and, using the car as a support, I stood picking the bits of glass from my wine-sodden clothes. An innocent bystander rushed over to me.

"That was a nasty fall," he said.

"Yes, I must agree with you there," was all I could think of to say until the smell of my clothing and type of shop from which I had come from prior to my fall brought more words, "I'm not hurt though and there's not a drop of blood."

"You were very lucky," he said. Then, leaning quite close, added in a sympathetic tone, "Is it MS?"

"Yes it is," I answered without a second thought. "It's a hell of a mess but it will soon dry up."

On hearing my answer, the man gave me a sad smile as he used his foot to brush the broken bottle into the gutter.

The pain in my back was now a little masked by other pains in my hands and knees but I had promised to deliver the panel and also a bottle of 'booze' so, after a minute's rest leaning on the car, I re-visited the 'Winery' and replaced the previous bottle.

On arrival at my destination, I was greeted with the news that the testing of the panel was not complete. I sat to wait for my colleague to finish his task, which took much longer than either of us had planned. By the time that the electrons were causing relays to close and lights to light in the correct sequence, it was past the closing time of our customers. However, I tried to contact them. I was surprised when I dialled their number on my friend's telephone to have it answered by the customer's Chief Engineer.

"Hello, Mr Worthington," he said when I had identified myself.

"You only just caught me. I wouldn't have been here but I've been in a Production Meeting all afternoon and it's only just broken up."

"I'm very glad I caught you," I sighed. "It's this panel we're making for you."

"Yes, I wanted to speak to you about that, Bob." (At the use of my Christian name I prepared myself for the worst.)

"We're behind on production and we don't need your panel for a fortnight."

"Oh, that's OK. It has been in our stores waiting to be delivered for a week, another two weeks won't make much difference."

I told him to have a pleasant weekend, hung up the 'phone and turned to my friend.

"Open that bottle – let's have a drink."

We had a drink. In fact, we emptied the bottle. My return drive was made (before breathalysers) in a lightly inebriated haze that hid every one of my aches and pains.

When I arrived home after the journey, during which I felt no pain, I found that I had (as I had feared I would last night whilst in bed) set like cement. Sylvia and Mum (who had arrived in my absence) released me from the car and, after a hot bath, 'laid me to rest' in bed. (I was to find, during these operations, that my mother had hidden talents, as did my wife, as a mortician). I was given food in this corpse-like position. I gave Sylvia my usual assistance with the Friday balance in this position and, in actual fact, I spent the following three days and the greater part of the following four nights in this position.

cHApTEr 17

My stay in bed finished on the next Tuesday morning when I was transferred downstairs to be laid out by my private undertakers on the settee in the living room. My pains had diminished greatly but I had almost enjoyed the intensive care that had been lavished on me the last few days. Sylvia had undertaken to attend to the bread man every day. Telephone calls had been made cancelling the cement delivery shortly after my arrival home on the previous Friday.

"It's a good thing you managed to get that panel delivered last Friday," Sylvia remarked during one of the few free moments she had had since I had taken to my bed.

"It's still in the car," I confessed, "but there's no need to worry about that. I 'phoned them from the university and told them that they could not have it until next week as my wife had ordered me to bed."

"You didn't, did you?" she snapped. "And what did they say?"

"Yes, I did. Ring them. And they said 'you should be so lucky'."

I don't think Sylvia believed me until she found the panel in the car boot, when she asked, "When do you plan to deliver it now?"

"Just as soon as you'll help me up from here."

"In that case your customer is due for a long wait."

My mother was of invaluable help during this period. Normally (at least during the working week), Sylvia had no time to exercise her culinary skills and so, since Marta's demise with her torte, paella and cod ball and chips, our table had only held mainly convenience foods. Mum reintroduced some of my childhood favourites – such delicacies as Scotch scallops, tripe and onions, fried tripe, tripe cooked in milk and potato cakes – the like of which was not to be found anywhere else. Mum always insisted that she did not cook, she 'concocted' and, brother, could she concoct!

On Friday, by which time after a week of total inactivity, my pains, if not completely gone, were bearable, my nurses allowed me to deliver the panel.

"You can take it provided you visit the doctor before returning home," was my mother's answer when I suggested that the drive would do me good.

If my wife had made this condition, I might have arrived home without fulfilling it. However, it was my Mother's wish so I had no choice but to obey. The doctor inspected the area of my body that gave me the majority of the pain and told me to rest for the next week or two.

"What did the doctor say?" I was asked by both members of my nursing staff almost before I had closed the door.

"He told me it's nothing to worry about. I've just got to take things easy for a couple of weeks, that's all," I reported.

I hoped that this news would ensure that I had a continuation of care and attention without any curtailment of my visits or, indeed, of whatever else I wanted to do.

My report of the visit to the general practitioner was accepted by my wife and mother. For the next week I was given consideration in all matters. I visited no customers and the only contact I made with industry was by telephone. I found no new business but I did manage to keep all existing customers reasonably happy.

The pain in my back diminished but did not disappear. Therefore, Mum returned to her home on the second weekend after deciding that her little boy was not about to 'pass on'. Because I was still having some difficulty, my remaining nurse asked me to give the doctor a further visit.

"I don't think they could do much to remove the pain except prescribe pain-killing pills and these would only hide the pain until their effects wore off," was my answer.

"Well, how about visiting an osteopath? Mrs Johnson told me in the shop this morning that her husband had a bad back for weeks and an osteopath put him right in a couple of seconds."

"Oh yes, I know, a couple of seconds of excruciating pain," I said. "If my pain gets any worse, I'll arrange to see one."

I decided I would cure my trouble myself without the help of the medics, either orthodox or unorthodox, and so I began a crash course in yoga. Years ago, I had practised this form of exercise for a number of months with very successful results. The period in time when I did 'the locust and the plough' and many of the other simple yoga postures was during the years shortly after the first show of MS when my spine was still supple. Only X-rays could have shown the condition of this important section of my skeleton when I began the 'asanas' now. I suppose that I still subscribed to the ridiculous theory that 'If it hurts, it must be doing you good'.

The results of my serious attempt to hold the 'plough' posture proved how ridiculous the theory is. I suggest that anyone unfamiliar with this yoga posture should lie flat on their back and, with a slow controlled movement, raise both legs over their body until the toes of both feet come into contact with the floor above their head — but please do not do it for the first time unless you are not suffering from anything more serious than a broken fingernail. Even then, it is imperative that you are under the instruction of a yoga teacher or at least a first-class osteopath.

My first efforts in this unusual attempt to cure a pain in the lower back proceeded with discomfort until I strained to put toes to the floor. The scream that followed a blinding flash of light behind my eyes and an indescribable stab of pain convinced my wife that I was mentally disturbed as well as physically disabled. It took her all her mortician's skill to straighten my abused body. My first question told her exactly how I was feeling.

"Did Mrs Johnson give you the 'phone number of the osteopath?"

"No, she didn't but I have no doubt it will be in the book."

"Please give him a ring and make an appointment for me and, if he is booked up till next year, tell him I'm not in a hurry," I added with my bravery decreasing in direct proportion to that of my exercise-induced extra pain.

Sylvia left me on the bathroom floor, the place I had chosen for my reintroduction to the postures of yoga.

"You're in luck," she called as she ran back up the stairs. "He said at first that he couldn't fit you in but, when I explained your trouble, he said he would see you at his surgery at eleven o'clock tonight."

"It isn't fair to jump the queue. Ring him back and tell him my pain has gone."

"Don't be silly. I'll get Mary to sit with the children so that I can come with you."

My wife can be very nasty and unlovable at times.

We arrived at the surgery at quarter to eleven. It was part of a large Victorian-style detached house. With Sylvia taking the place of my walking stick, we struggled up the three steps that led to a front door reminiscent of many seen in second feature mystery films. We pushed the button marked 'Please ring' and waited, can I say, a little nervously.

"If Tony Perkins in drag opens this door, don't forget you'll have to answer to my mother if you desert me," I said in a vain attempt to ease my tension.

The door opened smoothly and silently.

"Mr and Mrs Worthington?"

The tone of his voice made it into a question. I was prepared to say, "No. Could you direct us to the fire station," but Sylvia beat me.

"Yes, we are. I'm afraid we are early."

"No, you're not. You're just in time."

The osteopath turned and, as we accompanied him along a short passageway, we passed an older man coming out; he was ostentatiously carrying a heavy canvas corset he obviously no longer had a use for. Encouraged by this (what I hoped was an unsolicited testimonial), I followed the osteopath into his examination room. He sat at a small desk which, with two chairs and an upholstered manipulating table, made up the furniture in the room.

"Where's my wife gone?" I quickly asked on seeing that Sylvia had not followed us into the room.

"She will be waiting in the room next door, I expect," he answered.

As he wrote my answers to the many questions he asked on a card he had taken from a drawer in the desk, I studied the man.

To just say he was big would be an understatement. He was huge – his physique was that of a front-row forward or a heavyweight wrestler. In fact, I christened him 'Mick McManus' there and then. He was referred to this name by every member of my family from that day forward. On completing my interrogation he stood up.

"Please take all your clothes off except your underpants," he politely asked.

I immediately began to do as he requested, feeling more puny and undernourished with each piece of clothing I removed. (His biceps flexed would have a similar measurement to my chest expanded.) When my clothing was reduced to that most unglamorous of male apparel, I awaited his next instruction.

"Sit on the edge of the table," he instructed.

When I was perched on the table with my sparrow-like legs hanging freely over the side, he walked to the side of the table behind me. He made polite conversation as he examined my sensitive back. It was a one-sided conversation as the only thing of which I was conscious was his gentle but firm hand exploring the bones that made up my spine. After a few minutes of this inspection he gave his diagnosis. He told me there were four faults in the assembly of my body's bones, three of these I could not pronounce, let alone spell. The fourth one, of which I had heard, was a slipped disc.

"Thank you very much, sir," I said, climbing carefully down prepared to put my clothes on and go home.

"No, Mr Worthington. Get back onto the table and lie flat on your tummy. I can straighten you up quite easily."

I assumed the position he had suggested and he commenced to massage my back. The sensation was very pleasant but came to an end all too soon.

"Now roll over onto your back."

As he gave me this instruction, he walked to the foot of the table. When I had managed to roll over, he took hold of my left leg and, after moving it slowly in circles, he pulled it towards himself with considerable force. I was too surprised at his action to even cry out. He looked down at the position of my legs.

"Yes, they look better now," he decided.

From the position the rest of my body was in, the only thing I felt sure of was that my left leg was at least one foot longer than my right. Whilst I was endeavouring to feel if any permanent damage had been done to the joints where my left leg joined my torso, Mr McManus casually walked to the left side of the table.

"Now just relax," he advised me as he intertwined my arms and legs in a manner I am still sure was impossible. When the knot he had tied met with his approval, he gripped my right wrist in one of his enormous hands, placed his other hand against my bent left knee and snatched with his right hand and pushed with his left.

The split second of pain was more intense than spoken words can tell. My cry of pain emitted from my lungs a full second after the pain that brought it forth was a thing of the past.

"Sit facing me," he ordered as my deranged mind fought to make sense of the punishment this mountain of a man was inflicting on me.

I sat up trembling and still with the ache in my back. I put my arms around his neck and rested my head on his bulging shoulder. Involuntary tears rolled down my cheeks.

"Only one more," he said. "Then you will feel the difference."

"Do whatever you have to," I groaned.

I was past caring. My torturer took my arms from around his shoulder and went round the table to stand at my back. His soothing voice never ceased, not even when he put his arms below mine and clasped his hands at the back of my neck. (In wrestling circles this hold, I believe, is a classic – the full Nelson.) With no warning, he lifted me clear from the table and then gave my spine a movement that, if it had been a whip, it would have cracked. Once more the scream was a second too late for the pain.

"Oh, I'm sorry but it didn't go back in that time," he apologised.

Before I had time to say, 'Whatever it is, leave the bloody thing out,' he repeated his whip movement. I landed with a bump on the table and experienced a feeling of such relief that I believed I was in the presence of a wizard. All my pain had gone. It was magical. I jumped down from the table and even my walk seemed to be steadier. No way was I cured of MS but the relief from my back pain almost made me not care a hoot. I put my clothes on much more easily than I had shed them and looked at the osteopath with reverence.

"I want you to go home now and have a hot bath and take things very easily for a couple of days."

Sylvia joined me from the waiting room and, within half an hour, I was sitting in the hot bath whilst Sylvia quizzed me as to the reason for the screams she had heard emanating from the examination room.

"Examination room be damned! That's a torture chamber. Didn't you see his certificates on the walls? He's got three honours degrees, two from concentration camps."

"Did he really hurt you?" Sylvia asked in her most sympathetic voice.

"Yes, love, he did. But look, he can work miracles," I replied, demonstrating my lack of pain by moving to and fro.

"Now that's enough of that," she said, noticing a twinkle in my eye. She ran from the bathroom.

cHApTEr 18

I slept that night in the corpse-like position. Not that I had any pain but I felt extremely fragile. This feeling stayed with me for the next five days, during which time I made no sudden movements and ensured that I did not receive even the slightest knock. After those five days, however, my concentration waned. I bumped my hip against a bookcase and the pain returned. I was distraught, not so much because of the pain itself as from the thoughts of a second visit to the osteopath and his 'catch as catch can' treatment.

I gave much thought to the 'full Nelson with throw' that Mick had performed during my recent bout with him. I came to the conclusion that the principal object of this was to stretch my spine and it seemed obvious to me that I could achieve this objective by suspending myself in a hanging position. The prospect of another two or three rounds with Mr McManus made my alternative treatment appear very attractive. If the conclusion to my deliberations had meant hanging by the neck I would have given it serious consideration. However, the hanging, I had concluded, which would remove my back pain was hanging from my hands.

I searched through the whole of our property to find a suitable point from where I could suspend my thin frame. The only place I found that had the necessary requirements, the main one being that of height, was in Sylvia's shop. (If I did not want my feet to reach the floor before my spine had received the full benefit of my suspension.) The main beam along the ceiling held a row of hooks. We assumed that, once, 'sides' of salted pork and bacon had hung from these; this assured me that they were capable of holding my weight.

I had not informed Sylvia of my plans to enter the field of bone manipulation so I went into the shop and, as she served a couple of customers, I studied the hooks. There were two conveniently placed for my intended 'hanging'. They were above an area of floor that held none of the shop furniture. In fact, it was the spot where I was standing watching the postmistress serve (and gossip) with the village housewives. The last customer was attended to and she left. Sylvia turned to me.

"If you're going to stand there, I may as well go and prepare tonight's meal."

"OK, pet. I'll look after the shop for you," I agreed.

"If anyone comes in, give me a call," she said as she left me alone with the hooks.

I reached up and found that the tips of my fingers were three or four inches short so I considered jumping but knew that the jar my spine would suffer on land-ing would doubtless put me back into bed. I then noticed the set of two steps that Sylvia used to reach goods from the uppermost shelves. These were perfect. I moved them to the space below the hooks and, exercising the utmost caution, I climbed up the two steps. I was too high now but, gripping the hooks firmly, I slowly bent my knees until the weight of my upper body was supported in the manner I desired. The pain felt easier. Now, if I could move the steps to let my feet fall free I would have achieved my objective. I slowly took my feet off the steps and, with a swinging movement, the steps slipped across the floor to leave me slowly swinging but totally suspended. The relief was immediate and I was completely at ease. The only discomfort I was experiencing was in my hands gripping the old and rough surfaces of the iron hooks. 'Must be careful my hands don't slip' I was thinking when the shop door opened and in walked one of my wife's less favourite customers.

"Good afternoon, Mrs Denry. Sylvia won't be a minute." As I spoke, I tried to increase the arc of my movements but I could not reach the discarded steps.

Mrs Denry watched me in silence, unable to see the steps which were hidden behind the counter.

After a final unsuccessful lunge in the direction of the steps that had left me to swing like a pendulum and, suspended from hands that had begun to give me pain as severe as my now absent back pain, I decided to call for the assistance of the postmistress.

"Sylvia, there's a customer here," I called, giving up my struggles to painlessly reach the floor.

"I won't be a moment," came back my wife's answer from the kitchen.

"It's OK. I'm not in a hurry," interrupted Mrs Denry who, apparently mesmerised by my oscillations from side to side, had misunderstood the assistance we needed.

"I'd be pleased if you would come immediately," I countered.

My arms, as well as my hands, were beginning to feel the strain of my less than usual position.

"I'm coming," Sylvia grumbled as she walked from the kitchen.

She entered the shop through the door from our living quarters, glanced at me before giving the other occupant the sweetest smile.

"What on earth are you doing now?" Her question was directed at me although her eyes were directed to her patiently waiting customer. Before either the customer or I could answer the question, my once understanding wife continued, "And if you say 'You're just hanging around', just consider that you are in no position to defend yourself."

"Don't try to be smart and just put those steps under my feet so that I can climb down."

"I will not do anything until you give a solemn promise to see the doctor."

"No," I said defiantly. "Whilst I'm hanging here there is no pain in my back."

"As you wish," my mean, wicked spouse said. Then she spoke to the bemused, waiting Mrs Denry. During the whole discussion with me, Sylvia's eyes had remained on the lady. "Hello, what was it you wanted please." Without a pause and without turning her eyes from her customer, she again addressed me, "Doctor's – or you'll be feeling a bit hungry by this time tomorrow and I absolutely refuse to spoon feed you whilst you're swinging from a beam."

"Could I have my bread," chipped in Mrs Denry, managing to interrupt.

"The kids will feed me, even if you won't," I shouted.

Sylvia put the loaf of bread on the counter. "Is that all you want?" This to the customer. The remainder of her words were to me, even though they were said in an uninterrupted flow and without movement of head or eyes. "And next time use good, strong rope."

"I wanted a few other things but I can see this isn't a convenient moment. I'll pop back later," Mrs Denry said, moving towards the door.

"No, don't go Mrs Denry. Make her serve you," I strongly suggested but Mrs Denry ignored me, giving Sylvia an understanding smile as she quietly closed the shop door behind her.

"Well, you've lost a customer there," I attacked.

"I should be so lucky. I've been trying to get rid of her for months."

I could see my wife had the 'bit' firmly between her teeth and the pain in my hands was, by this time, bordering on the unbearable so, as Sylvia moved in the direction of the kitchen, I relented.

"As a matter of fact, I intend to go to the doctor's tomorrow anyway so you may as well help me down."

"When are you going to the doctor's did you say?"

"This afternoon — and for God's sake get me down quick. My hands are about to burst into flame."

I'll say this for my wife, she accepts defeat very well. So, very quickly, my feet were returned to the floor and, just as quickly, the pain returned to my back.

I visited our doctor within an hour of my release and, unbelievably, received immediate audience. My symptoms and the location and severity of my pains were discussed at length, after which I confessed to a crime I had been led to believe would alienate any and all doctors from its perpetrators.

"I've been to an osteopath," I said with my eyes downcast.

"Have you?"

Now for the reprimand, I thought.

"If I had a bad back, I'd go to an osteopath. Didn't he help you?"

"Oh yes, but not permanently," I replied, relieved that I wasn't to have my wrists slapped.

"I think it would be wisest to have your back X-rayed to see if there is anything damaged in your spine," the doctor concluded.

And so, a few days later, I visited the nearest general hospital where all parts of my body were subjected to 'see through' rays. I was recalled to this hospital within a further few days to be told the results of the photographs. I was, in fact, shown the negative of my 'snap' covering, or rather uncovering, the section of my torso from neck down to hips. The doctor who was holding this negative to the light and so illuminating my bones went to great lengths to point out that near to the base of my spine (I was later to learn the correct medical term was lumbar regions) the bones were a little scrambled.

"This is what is known as a stress fracture of the lumbar vertebrae caused by osteoporosis. There are also some signs of slight osteoarthritis," he explained.

I carefully studied the area of the negative he indicated.

"I bet that's the reason I've got a pain in my back," I stated.

"I think you are possibly right there, Mr Worthington," he said, lowering the X-ray print from the light.

"Well, do you operate?" I asked bravely.

The doctor smiled. "No, I am afraid there is nothing we can do along those lines. However, we can fit you up with a corset that will relieve the pressure on the damaged part of your spine and that should stop the pain."

Pleased that I wasn't to come under the knife, I asked if he would lead me to the hospital's corsetiere.

"You will have to come back tomorrow. The people you want to see are only in the hospital on one day a week."

I attended, as suggested, the following day to be measured for my new garment and, again, I attended two weeks later to collect my made-to-measure back support system. During this fortnight, I saw my own doctor who prescribed some pain-killing drugs and also my specialist who, after telling me I appeared obese, 'took me off' Synactin Depot.

I arrived home from the third visit to the hospital and quickly donned my new corsets. I learned within minutes the reason why overweight ladies slim if the alternative to loss of weight means the wearing of this type of instrument of torture. I began to eat the pain-relieving tablets like pig strawberries, mainly to ease the pain that accompanied the wearing of the corset. It was about a week before the pain-killing drugs took their fullest effects. They had killed the pain within minutes of my swallowing them but it took a week before their main side effect came to the fore or, as in my case, came to the rear, introducing me to a totally new pain in a totally different part of my anatomy.

The Wednesday of the week following my succumbing to the painkillers dawned to find me sitting on the 'loo'. Strain as I might and with all my might, accompanying myself with my full repartee of grunts and groans (greatly widened over the past weeks), I was unable to 'place my faeces'. I was solid.

The day slowly passed and, throughout it, I remained on the throne. Sylvia came to the foot of the stairs at half past five that evening, after closing the shop.

"Any movement yet?" she called.

I was feeling more than a little distressed from the several hours of unrewarded strain.

"Nothing!" I snapped with a pain that I was sure indicated a cannonball was lodged in the entrance of my back passage. "I am sure this is more than constipation," I complained.

"Have you passed any water?" she enquired.

"Not since about mid-morning, I think, but I've not been keeping any records."

"Then I'm ringing the doctor."

I shouted an objection which my wife chose to ignore and she disappeared to contact our general practitioner. In a few minutes, Sylvia reappeared and started to ascend the stairs.

"I've spoken to the doctor and he is sending an ambulance for you."

"I'm not going to hospital," I stated definitely and loudly.

"You are," Sylvia stated equally definitely and more than twice as loud.

I offered no further argument as the size of the cannonball had increased as we were speaking and I admitted to myself that, for once, my wife was correct.

cHApTEr 19

It seemed only a few moments before, once more, I heard Sylvia running up the stairs, calling me as she came, "The ambulance is here. Are you ready?"

"No, I've told you I am not going to hospital," I answered.

"Now don't be stupid. Jane's just opening the door for them now; they will be up here in a minute."

"If they want me to go anywhere, they'll have to carry me," I announced defiantly.

"I think they are quite prepared for that. I expect they have brought a stretcher with them."

"Well tell them I don't need their stretcher; I'm not a cripple. I'm quite capable of walking to the ambulance."

As I was saying this, the first of the ambulance men appeared at the foot of the staircase and had obviously heard my words.

"I think it would be much safer if we did use the stretcher. We don't want you tumbling down these stairs, now do we?"

"And what makes you so sure that I won't roll off the stretcher? You're not to know but if I hit the floor with a bump I might explode and blow us all to pieces," I informed him.

A puzzled look came to his face and, before he could think of another argument, with Sylvia's help I eased myself onto my feet and slowly and with very great care I descended the 13 steps.

I was only dressed in my dressing gown, without even pyjamas, as my reign on the throne had started minutes after rising from my bed that morning. The ambulance men had both been arranging the stretcher on the floor at the bottom of the stairs and, as soon as I gingerly lowered myself from the bottom step, I was picked up without so much as a 'by your leave' by the two men and laid onto the waiting stretcher.

"Not on my back, please not on my back," I pleaded as they performed their well-rehearsed task.

I felt absolutely sure that the cannonball would be ejected with great force at any moment. I was afraid, not only of the pain that would accompany its 'firing', but the unthinkable mess it would make wherever it came to rest. Strapped to the stretcher, I was easily carried by my two attendants. They slid and then locked me into position in the ambulance. Sylvia climbed in after arranging with Mary (who had arrived more or less at the same time as the ambulance) to take care of both our children. I could see a small group of villagers standing around our car park, making the most of the unusual sight and the excitement of an ambulance at the post office. I was struggling into a position, from which I could give them my version of a 'royal wave' to acknowledge their concern, when the rear doors of the vehicle were closed on us.

"I've 'phoned Glenys," Sylvia informed me, "and she's coming over right away so you've no need to worry about Jane and Jamie."

I was to feel very ashamed of my behaviour within a few hours but, at that exact moment, I was concerned about nothing else but my 'cannonball', the pain it gave me and the definite possibility, nay likelihood, of its ejection.

"That's good but are you sure the driver knows the smoothest route to the hospital? I should have told him there's a nasty bump in the road just opposite the railway station."

"I'm sure he will know every bump in the road for miles around the hospital," she said in an effort to calm me.

The trouble was she wasn't aware of the amount of pain I was in or the imminent danger we were all in!

"Do you think I should shout to him?" I asked.

Sylvia didn't answer but stood up and looked through the darkened window.

"You needn't worry about that bump; we're well past the station. In fact, we are just about to turn into the hospital now."

We felt the vehicle make a sharp turn and, after a few more seconds of travel, it came to rest. The doors of the ambulance were opened and, still on the stretcher, I was quickly withdrawn, placed on a trolley and pushed through the already-open doors of the entrance clearly marked 'Emergencies Only'. I travelled down a passage at a speed that had Sylvia trotting behind in order to keep up with us. We were conducted into an 'Inspection' room, followed by a doctor and a nurse.

"Now where is the pain?" the doctor asked as he opened the front of my dressing gown and placed both his hands on my tummy.

"You're at the wrong side," I advised him, "but could you please give me something to kill the pain."

"Not just yet," he answered and began to question me in detail about my bowels and whether I was taking any type of medication.

Between moans and groans, I was doing my utmost to give answers to his questions when an older doctor joined us and, after listening to my answer, he stepped up to my stretcher, gently but firmly rolled me over onto my stomach and, with the bravery of a bomb-disposal officer, he pushed one of his digits right up my rectum.

"Give me something to kill the pain," I howled.

My pleas were completely ignored by the doctor who remained attached to me. Without using actual words, I made it noisily very clear that the doctor's invasion of my person was not welcome. I looked to my wife for help but my once-beloved spouse had taken a position as far from me as possible and wore the expression of a complete stranger.

"All this man needs is an enema," he declared above the noise of my distress as he withdrew his finger and walked from the room followed by all the hospital staff.

They left only Sylvia to listen to my complaints. I calmed down a little, that is until I saw that my wife had crouched slightly and was adjusting her hair, using the chromium-plated side of a piece of hospital equipment as a mirror. No-one seemed to care or to understand the intense pain I was suffering.

"Get some attention for me," I ordered after a number of minutes had passed since the doctors and nurses had left us.

Sylvia didn't answer and continued with her hairdressing. At this, I saw red.

"OK then, I'll get some help myself," I said and began to shout, "Help, Help!"

At my third call, the door burst open and in rushed more than enough doctors and nurses.

"I'll attend to him on the ward," said the doctor who had first examined me on arrival. "Get him admitted."

"First give me something to kill the pain," I begged without any response.

Everyone present appeared to have forgotten about me and my cannonball as they carried out their duties. I considered rolling over and carefully pointing myself at someone as I was sure the ejection must be imminent now. One of the nurses separated herself from her colleagues and walked over to me. 'Action at last,' I thought.

"I'm the registrar," she smilingly announced.

Before she could say more I asked, "Do your duties involve issuing drugs?"

"No," she answered and quickly continued, "What is your religion?"

"My religion is open-minded about taking drugs, at least for medical reasons any way."

"The quicker you answer my questions the quicker you will receive attention."

Normally I would have given the lady an argument about this bartering of medical attention for personal information but I really was in pain so I answered, "I'm C of E and I intend to write to my MP if I get out of here."

I had answered the rest of her questions when I noticed one of the doctors leading Sylvia from the room.

"Sylvia, don't let them take you away," I called.

"There's no need to worry, Mr Worthington," the registrar said quietly. "She will see you when we get you on the ward."

"Are you sure about that? And my name is Worthington," I groaned.

A new nurse appeared as the registrar left. This nurse had the build of a lady wrestler (probably related to Mick) and, before I had time to ask her for the painkiller I needed, she had pushed another trolley to the side of the one on which I lay.

"Come on now, we don't want any babies here. Over onto that trolley."

"That's all I'm short of, a bloody bully," I snapped angrily.

The amazon smiled and gently lifted me bodily and transferred me to the second trolley.

Two nurses wheeled me into a ward that already contained 15 or 16 men, all sitting tidily, awaiting the arrival of friends and relatives as the visiting hour was about to start. The doctor arrived and stood behind the trolley where I lay.

"Get him into bed," he said. "I'll see him after visiting time."

I was hastily 'womanhandled' into a vacant bed and, before I could plead for drugs, the doors at the end of the ward swung open.

A procession of people entered, bearing gifts of flowers and the type of presents that I am sure are carried into wards of all hospitals in the over-developed countries of the world. None of them were of the least interest to me, unless one of my fellow patient's visitors had been a drug pusher. The last person to enter the ward through the doors was Sylvia. She glided up the middle of the ward between the rows of beds. I was sure she was pretending that the groaning patient in my bed was a total stranger to her. I called to her, without sympathy for the embarrassment I was causing her. My unkind thoughts were false. When she heard her name called between my moans and groans, she ran over to me and sat on the chair provided at the side of my bed.

"How are you Bob?" she asked.

"I wish they would give me something to kill this pain but they are not going to do anything until after visiting time."

"You'll be OK," she said in a tone that suggested she was not enjoying the many looks we were getting from other people in the crowded ward.

"Don't worry about them," I said and increased the volume and frequency of my groans. "None of them have a cannonball stuffed up their anus."

"Don't talk so loudly," Sylvia requested.

I didn't speak again until around 10 minutes later when a wave of nausea caused me to believe that the cannonball was seeking a different exit.

"Quick, I'm going to be sick. Get me a bowl," I cried.

Away poor Sylvia ran, loudly calling for a bowl. She returned at speed, pursued by a nurse who carried a large white enamel bowl.

My feeling of nausea had passed almost as quickly as it had appeared so that when the bowl and its attendants arrived at my bedside I snapped, "You can take that away. I no longer need it."

The look in the two pairs of eyes that greeted my words made me sure that a large white enamel bowl was about to join my cannonball. The only doubt was through which of my body's two main passages it would be forced. I once more increased the volume of my groans in a successful attempt to dissuade the two females from taking this action.

The remainder of the visiting time passed in near silence but I would not let Sylvia leave me until she had promised, and the nursing staff had agreed, that she would not leave for home until my 'operation' had been completed.

My wife was not detained at the hospital for long. The 'operation' was all over in 10 minutes. The doctor who performed it never even approached that part of my body that housed the cannonball. 'The bomb disposal officer must be off watch,' I thought. A young nurse had held my hand whilst the doctor fed yards of plastic tubing into the small opening at the working end of my penis. When he was satisfied with the length of tubing he had threaded into me, he stood back and watched as a great amount of fluid drained from me into a plastic bag that had been clipped to the frame of my bed.

"Did that hurt, Mr Warrington?" he asked.

"Not at all — and my name's Worthington," I croaked.

"That's good," he said proudly. "I'm told I do that painlessly."

I wondered who had given him this information and whether he boasted of his prowess to his friends but, as the cannonball had still to be removed, I made no impertinent comment. I had no wish to antagonize the person who was likely to perform this delicate part of my operation. I decided instead to try once more for relief from my still-present pain.

"Can I please have something to ease my pain?"

"Of course," he answered and, turning to one of the nurses, he instructed her as to which drug was suitable and the amount to inject into me.

The nurse carried out the instructions and the cannonball dissolved. My wife was led back to my bedside.

"Do you feel a little better now, love?" she asked, looking far more weary than the much- requested drug had left me.

"I'm fine, pet. But you don't look at all well. If I were you I'd get an early night then perhaps you'll feel better tomorrow."

"Don't worry about me. Just get better and come home as soon as you can," she said and, giving me a motherly kiss on my forehead, she walked from the ward.

With my wife on her way back to the home and family, I lay back onto the pillows and enjoyed the freedom from any pain. In a state of euphoria that the drug had induced, I absorbed my unfamiliar surroundings. I saw that a set of headphones hung at the head of every bed and assumed that there would be a set behind my bed but, try as I might, I could not reach them so I closed my eyes and drifted into sleep.

I was gently awoken and opened my eyes to find a nurse bending over me.

"Wake up, Mr Warrington."

"You've got the wrong man; my name's Worthington. Goodnight," I whispered and closed my sleep-filled eyes.

"No matter what your name is, I have got to give you an enema. It's not very pleasant for me either but it has got to be done," she stated sternly.

(I was to find that when she carried out this most objectionable operation that, without doubt, her part of the procedure was worse than mine.)

I had never been subjected to anything remotely approaching an enema before. At first, I began to think that the nurse was insane.

"Look Miss, if that's medicine, isn't it more usual to take it by mouth?"

"Please be quiet, Mr Warrington, before you wake up the whole ward," she said as she continued to pour liquid into a funnel that led up my rear passage.

"The name's Worthington. Why? What time is it?" I asked at the same time that I noticed it was dark outside the window. With only two small lights illuminating the ward, it was not much lighter inside.

"Around 2.30 am," she barked.

"At this time all good children should be asleep," I suggested.

"Please, Mr Warrington, at least try to help me," she said in a much kinder voice.

"OK, Miss, you seem to be a nice girl really. If you will call me Mr Worthington, I'll come with you into the bathroom and, if you fill the bath with water, I'll drown myself the easy way," I said in despair.

"Is your name really Worthington?"

"Yes, it really is," I answered. "I wish you would stop pouring when you speak."

"Well it says Warrington on your chart."

As she spoke, the substance that had been contained in the cannonball burst forth from the entrance to my body into which she had been pouring the liquid. I had no control over this expulsion.

"I did ask you to stop, didn't I?" I said to the poor girl who had had no more warning than I.

"Don't be upset, Mr Warrington. I'm used to this sort of thing," she endeavoured to console me but I was still feeling no pain, only acute embarrassment.

"What a funny sort of life you must lead. And please alter that blasted chart – I swear my name is not Warrington."

The nurse cleaned me with the care a mother would her baby. She changed all the bedclothes, which was none too easy as I was still attached by a thin plastic tube to the bed frame. However, she was a true professional and, within half an hour, she left me in a clean bed whilst she disappeared out of the ward — to have a bath I hoped. I could no longer sleep again and relived the past 24 hours that had passed with the speed of a week.

The nurse walked back up the ward as the first streaks of daybreak were lightening the windows.

"Are you all right now, Mr Worthington?" she politely asked.

I was very tempted to claim my name was Warrington but I realised that I had given this girl, as well as everyone else I had come into contact with during those 24 hours, more than enough trouble.

"Yes, I'm perfect now, nurse. Thank you very much for all you've done for me. For your sake, I hope we never have to meet again," I said in an effort to apologise.

"You'll see me again tonight. I'm on nights all this week."

"But I'll be going home tomorrow."

"I don't know for sure but I will be surprised if you go home this week."

I smiled, believing I knew best, but doubt increased and I suddenly realised that I had no money with me, not even one penny, so I called the nurse back.

"I don't like to ask but could you possibly lend me some money? I forgot to bring any with me. I'll pay you back tonight."

I couldn't blame her when she replied, smiling, "But Mr Worthington, I thought you said you were going home today."

I was saved from being totally outwitted when I remembered my exact words and had untangled yesterday, today and tomorrow in my head.

"To be correct, I said I would be going home tomorrow and my name is Warburton."

"OK, you win. Will half a crown be enough and, if you can arrange not to be here tonight, you can keep it."

cHApTEr 20

When the night nurse had left me with the coin she had loaned me in my hot little hand (clutched like a small child's first penny), I settled back and dozed away what little was left of the night.

I was awakened as the hospital day nurses began their day's duties. I was immediately aware that the coin held firmly in my hand was not the main reason I felt like an infant. Something had happened in my bed. I was sure this had not happened for many, many years but it was something that was to happen again during the following day. It was ironical – yesterday I spent the full day endeavouring to do the one thing that I now found I could do in my sleep.

"Nurse, nurse!" I called.

A nurse who, unfortunately for her, was hurrying down the ward, stopped and walked over to me.

"Good morning, Mr Warrington. Something wrong?"

I accepted my new name without comment because I was so embarrassed. It was unnecessary to confess as to what was wrong as the nauseating aroma was very prevalent when she stood at the foot of my bed.

"Deary me, have you had an accident? Still, you had an enema during the night, didn't you?"

"Yes nurse," I answered sadly.

"Well don't let it upset you. It's quite normal. Someone will come to sort you out as soon as we get organised." She smiled at my obvious relief and carried on with her duties.

I waited for an hour before the nurses were organised and one approached me.

"I have just received the details from your own doctor and it says you have Multiple Sclerosis."

"Yes, but that's not the reason I was brought here."

"I know that," she boasted, looking at the chart that had been hung on my bed. "Why have you been telling everyone your name is Warrington? You should have known we would find out your real name sooner or later."

"I've never told anyone my name is Warrington. I asked the night nurse to alter the chart last night but she must have forgotten."

"The chart has been changed but there are other records that your silliness has upset. So, in future, answer all questions truthfully," she lectured. "Now let's get you cleaned up and, if you want to move your bowels again, shout one of the nurses and they will bring you a wheelchair."

She drew the curtains around my bed and had just begun her unpleasant task when another nurse pushed her head through the curtains and said, "You'll have to leave that. Mr Hornby is here. He's doing his rounds early today."

The bedclothes were thrown back over me, the curtains drawn open and the nurses rushed down to the bottom of the ward to join a group of four doctors assembled around the bed nearest to the door. I waited as the collection of medics drew nearer and nearer to my bed until they stood around me.

Dr Hornby studied my clipboard and then, turning to the nurse closest to him, said, "I don't think his enema has done its work – give him another." He smiled at me as if he had just presented me with first prize in a raffle and led his entourage to the next patient.

I had to wait until the doctors had looked at all the other patients in the ward before they left and two young nurses approached and drew the curtains around my bed. After cleaning away the mess resulting from the last one, they treated me to another enema. This time, the person who received the fruits of their labours was a very attractive young student nurse; she really was something else. I have no doubt she figured large in the night-time fantasies of any male patient who consider nurses in uniform number one. Later that day, I was to discover that her only flaw was a slight speech impediment when, as she passed my bed, I heard her singing softly to herself a popular song of the time.

"Oh you chitty, chitty, bang, bang."

I decided, on hearing her, that she must have some difficulty in pronouncing her soft 'c', she made it sound similar to the 's' in shower.

The day passed very slowly. I had bought a morning newspaper with my borrowed money. One of my fellow patients handed me my earphones which the pain in my back prevented me from reaching for myself, and I began an affair with Radio 4 that has continued to this day. Three times I was provided with food, none of which I ate. Not that it was cold or foul-smelling or totally unappetizing in appearance but because I was working on the theory that the less I put in at one end the less there would be to come out at the other. My theory proved effective until a few seconds before the visitors were due.

"Nurse, nurse, quick, quick! . . . No need to run, you are too late."

There were loud calls from every other man, every one of whom were preparing to see their loved ones.

The nurse, who I had earlier learned was the sister in charge, stood with her back to the closed doors, thereby preventing any visitor from entering the ward.

"Silence!" she shouted, sounding like a sergeant major addressing noisy troops.

"Mr Warrington, you'll have to wait until the visitors have gone," she said more quietly to me.

There was a murmur of approval from the ranks. I could understand this response from the completely bedridden but I was surprised that the walking wounded were willing to subject their beloveds to half an hour in my air space which they knew to be unpleasant. (In fact, a number of them had given up eating that day as the table where they were expected to sit and eat their meals stood a few feet from the foot of my bed.) Sister turned, opened the door and in flooded the tide of families and friends. Amongst them walked Sylvia and sister Glenys.

"How are you?" they asked in unison.

"It's OK now but most of the people here are utter nutters. They're not even sure who I am. How are the children?"

"Jane was a little upset at first but they were both better when Glen said she would stay the night," Sylvia informed me whilst my sister went to collect an extra chair as only one had been provided.

"Before I forget, have you got any money on you? I had to borrow some from one of the nurses."

"No, I haven't a penny with me," Sylvia replied. "Glenys will have some, I expect."

Glenys had just returned but had not sat down on her chair when Sylvia interrupted,

"Have you any money? Bob hasn't got any and he owes a nurse some."

My sister patted her pockets. "Not a bean but there's some in the car. I'll go and get it."

Immediately, she spun round and, at a fast trot, she hurried through the ward doors. Sylvia waited a couple of seconds before she leapt to her feet too.

"She'll never make it, the car park is about half a mile away," she said, almost to herself. She then followed my sister at an even faster jog.

"Come back, you've only got 30 minutes," I called after my wife as she disappeared through the doors.

I sat back in the bed and its contents, held up my arms and looked around smilingly at the patients and visitors. Every face in the ward turned first to me and then slowly to the doors which were gradually swinging closed after the rapid exit of my visitors. Then, slowly, they looked back to me. In unison, all the visitors turned back to the patients at whose bedside they sat, leaned forward over their beds and filled the air with whispered questions that collectively sounded like thunder to me. I was never to learn any of the explanations that were given that night as to the reason for my visitors' actions but I spent the next 20 minutes straining my ears, hoping to catch a snippet of conversation.

With 10 minutes of visiting time remaining, my visitors returned and, once more, every face in the ward watched as they walked from the door back to my bed, perhaps checking to see if they were wearing oxygen masks! I was given a pound note, the only money my sister had found in the car. This was far more than I had borrowed and should have settled my debt but the night nurse had no change.

"Look, Mr Whatsit, my offer still stands. If you can work your discharge tomorrow you can still keep it," she said when I tried to settle my account with her later that night.

I slept like the proverbial log throughout my second night in hospital and awoke refreshed and, more importantly, clean. I am sure that I would have been released that day but for my desire to listen to Radio 4. A nurse, unfortunately, observed my painful attempts to reach the earphones. She quickly came to my assistance.

"Are you having difficulty in getting them?" she asked as she handed them to me.

"Just a little pain when I twist my back," I replied. "Nothing to worry about."

She made no comment and left me after checking that I could hear the programme of my choice. I realised later that she had 'grassed' on me to her superiors when, a short time later, a different nurse came to my bedside pushing a stretcher trolley.

"Get on here, Mr Worthington, please."

"Why, where are you taking me?"

"You have to go to the X-ray Department," I was informed.

"That's ridiculous! I was X-rayed only a couple of weeks ago," I complained.

"Please don't be difficult. I'm only doing as I am told to do."

"Me? Difficult? If you say I've got to go, then I'll go, but the bed will have to go with us. Remember I'm still plumbed to it."

"Oh yes, I was forgetting," she admitted. "Sorry but I can't attend to that."

"Not to worry, I'll wait if you'll go and get the plumber."

The nurse left me and, a short time later, an older member of the hospital staff took her place. She drew the curtains and uncovered the lower half of my body, revealing the point where the plastic tube disappeared into my insides. I will admit that I had given a lot of thought as to the level of pain that would accompany the withdrawal of this pipe. The lady whose task it was to 'withdraw' was understanding and took hold of the plastic.

"Now do you want me to withdraw it slowly or with one quick pull?" she offered.

I answered by reaching down and, gripping her hand, with one steady pull I removed my connection with the bed.

"It didn't hurt, did it?" I was asked.

"It was most thrilling," I truthfully answered, pulling the sheet over my once private parts.

"You must lie quiet, drink as much water as you can and take the tablets I will bring you. We don't want any infection in there do we?"

"No, that is the last thing we want in there," I agreed.

Eventually, the first nurse returned and once more asked me to climb onto the trolley. With difficulty, I did as she requested and was then pushed down and along a number of passages until we arrived at the self-same department I had visited a couple of weeks earlier. The same radiologist took another set of photographs of me in the identical postures to those I had taken and held for 60 seconds on my previous visit.

"I'm afraid that light must have got into the last lot," I called to the radiologist as my nurse pushed me away to start our journey back to my bed.

We arrived in time for what was laughingly called lunch. I watched as all but the walking wounded devoured this substance masquerading as food. (The air around my bed still had traces of enema products.)

I had been promised a bath earlier in the day so, when I saw two nurses walking purposefully towards my bed, I felt sure they were coming to help me to the bathroom. I was wrong. They drew the curtains around my bed which separated me from the body of the ward. The nurse who appeared through the totally-drawn curtain was the young beauty I have previously described.

"I understand you want a bath," she said, giving me one of her sweetest smiles.

"I certainly do. Are you going to help me to the bathroom?"

"Sister has decided that it wouldn't be safe to leave you in the bathroom by your-self in case you fall."

"Just a minute, I bath myself all the time at home," I interrupted her.

"But you're our responsibility in here so Sister has told me you've to have a bed bath."

"And what does that entail?" I asked, not very politely.

"We wash you whilst you're in your bed of course," she answered as if she was speaking to a moron.

I must admit that, as this method of bathing was explained to me by this de-lightful young lady, some erotic thoughts began to pass through my mind. I completely controlled the baser side of my personality, however. This test of my moral character was made a little easier as, at the moment I was about to submit my body to this angel's tender wishes, through the curtains came the second nurse carrying a large bowl full to its brim with what I was to learn was water extremely close in temperature to that of ammonia in its solid state. This second nurse was also not exactly pretty.

I lay flat on my bed except for a towel spread over the centre section of my manly frame. Beauty and the Beast then washed me from my shoulders down to my waist and then upwards from the soles of my feet to a few inches above my knees. They then stood back from the bed and Nurse Quasimodo said, "That is all we are allowed to do. You must do the rest yourself."

I was astounded at this ruling. In the couple of days since I had been admitted to this mad house, I had had a man publicly stick his finger up my anus and another man feed plastic tubing down my penis (and this whilst a young lady held my hand). On two separate occasions, two different girls had stuck funnels where the first man (without asking my permission) had pushed his finger and then poured gallons of fluid into the mouth of the funnel. A number of females had cleaned from all parts of my person the mess that had followed, quite natu-rally I would have thought, this last performance.

It seemed most unfair that the two nurses who were giving me a bed bath were denied the more pleasant task of washing a reasonably clean male body. I was unable to convince just one of these nurses that, in the interest of nurse liberation, they should ignore this unjust order (no prizes for guessing which of the two I tried to convince) so I completed my own toiletries.

I enjoyed the full term of that evening visiting time when, this time, my wife brought Mary and, later, I enjoyed a second good night's sleep.

I was very determined that, no matter how well I was sleeping, the new dawning day was to be the day of my discharge. I didn't eat the food provided but breakfasted on some more acceptable titbits that my visitors of last evening had thoughtfully smuggled into my bedside locker.

I waited impatiently for the daily rounds of the doctors. Eventually, the doors at the bottom of the ward opened and through them came three men accompanied by an equal number of nurses. They arrived at my bed very quickly, as in one of the two beds between mine and the ward doors now lay a road accident casualty who had been admitted the previous night. He was the third patient brought into the ward during my short stay with serious injuries and the dreadful condition and uncomplaining suffering of these men caused me great embarrassment when I remembered my noisy arrival three days earlier.

The senior doctor stood at the foot of my bed studying the negatives that I assumed were the results of my latest visit to the hospital's X-ray Department.

"Well, Mr Worthington, I have your X-ray photographs here and they do not look very good."

"It's not too serious though, is it doctor." I stated more than asked.

"No," he answered, "but nothing that we should ignore."

I could tell from the tone of his voice that he was not thinking of granting my discharge and this affected my words and the manner in which they were spoken.

"Can I have a guess at what the photographs indicate?" The doctor gave me a puzzled look but did not give an answer to what, to him, was a very strange question so I continued, "The pain in my back has the definite feel of a stress fracture in my lumbar vertebrae, more than likely caused by osteoporosis and it feels as if there is possibly a little osteoarthritis as well."

The nurses appeared most surprised at the correct diagnosis that I had made of my back pain but the doctor was not fooled.

"Who told you the results of your X-ray," he demanded.

"I've been trying to tell your nurses that I had an X-ray two weeks ago and your colleagues in Outpatients were not quite as secretive as you appear to be. Now, if you have nothing new to tell me, I'm going home."

"I think that is the best thing to do," He concluded our discussion with these words and walked to the next patient.

"Could you bring me the telephone nurse?" I rudely called.

"You'll have to wait your turn, Mr Warrington, the telephone is in use," another nurse shouted from across the ward.

I deservedly was made to wait until all the other patients had used the instrument before the trolley that held it was pushed to me and I contacted Sylvia requesting transport to return me to the fold.

cHApTEr 21

As my wife was involved in her duties as sub-postmistress and village storekeeper, it fell to my sister to collect her favourite brother (I can claim this without fear of contradiction being her only sibling) from the hospital. She arrived within an hour of my telephone call, complete with my 'civvy' clothes, including one of my corsets. I managed to dress but found it impossible to fasten my trousers at the waist when my corset was in place. It was fortunate that the hospital staff insisted I was transported from the ward to my sister's car by wheelchair as one can easily imagine the difficulty encountered in walking with two walking sticks when no amount of willpower will hold up loose unsupported clothing.

"We haven't told Mum you have been in hospital," were Glenys's first words to me as she drove me from the hospital confines.

"That's nice," I said, understanding the reasons for withholding the information from my parent. Perhaps I had not been an ideal patient during my few days' stay but this action of my wife and sister, whilst having the main purpose of saving Mum from worry, without any shadow of doubt had saved the doctors and nurses of this particular hospital from a potential full-scale invasion from the most radical member of my family.

We arrived home and my immediate family appeared to be as pleased as I at my return. I was given lunch and then placed in an easy chair in front of the television with strict orders not to move.

Sylvia closed the shop a little earlier that evening, my sister left to return to her family and soon I was surrounded by a caring wife and two children, all intent on proving to me how happy they were to have the 'lord and master' back with them.

"Your Mum is coming tomorrow for the week," Sylvia informed me casually.

"When are you going to tell her I've been in hospital?" I asked, equally casually.

"She's your mother so I think you should tell her," she passed the buck.

"I don't think I'm strong enough yet, I've only just come out of hospital."

We need not have worried, as my mother, by some mysterious Sixth sense had, throughout my life, been able to read me like a book, no matter how firmly I endeavoured to keep the covers closed. Whether I played 'wag' from school, taken a fancy to a girl whom my Mum did not think worthy of her son or, as on this occasion, been rushed to hospital, Mother, with only one look at my face, would know. It has remained one of the mysteries of my life that she hadn't diagnosed MS long before I gave her the facts. (But then again, she probably had.)

"What have you been in hospital for?" were almost her first words on arrival the following morning.

"They just wanted to carry out a few more tests," I replied, hoping her second sight wouldn't see through my answer.

"And what did they find?" was her next question.

"I've just got to take things easy for a few days and eat as much tripe and onions and meat and potato pies as I can manage."

Mum accepted this report and very soon she was concocting a meal for us all.

"Why don't you have a few days' holiday?" she suggested as we were recovering after devouring her concoction.

"I'd love that," said Sylvia. "But we can't leave the shop. Can we?" she added, obviously hoping someone would make it possible.

"Of course you can" came back Mum, who I am sure had been plotting this since I was first laid out. "I'll ask someone to come and stay here with me to look after the property and I'm sure you can persuade Mary to attend to the shop for a week."

Sylvia, I could see, would not need persuading and looked to me for my reaction.

"What do you think?" I asked Sylvia, adding, "You know I'm putty in your hands. If you say we go, then I daren't object."

"Where can we go though?" Sylvia answered with a question that indicated the decision had been taken.

"Glenys and Les had a week's holiday at a small hotel in Llandudno a few years ago," Mum reminded us, "and a break there would do you all good."

"I bet we would never get in there," said Sylvia, obviously sold on the idea.

"There is only one way to find out," I decided and went to the telephone, first obtaining the details of the hotel from my sister.

From the speed with which she supplied all the details, I was even more convinced that we were victims of a pre-arranged plan. I telephoned the hotel and was informed that we were fortunate that they could offer us accommodation the very next week, provided we would share one bedroom with our two children. These sleeping arrangements were not as I would have chosen as I believed that the children's presence could possibly interfere with my night walks should my spine become rigid again. (Or any of the other desires that accompanies rigidity of the body!)

Every member of the family was overjoyed with the arrangement. Sylvia discussed our plans with Mary, who immediately agreed to take full control of our business with the exception of the 'balance'. We promised that we would not leave for our break until the following Sunday morning and would return on the Friday of the next week in ample time to undertake this task.

Mum departed and returned on the Saturday, accompanied by Mrs Partington, the better half of a pair of old family friends, and so we retired to bed for the final night's sleep before we were to start our first holiday since our MS inspired business life had begun two and a half years previously.

"I've never asked but how did you manage whilst I was in hospital?" I belatedly asked my wife as we settled down in bed that night.

"It was easy but only thanks to Glenys really," Sylvia answered.

"Yes, they're not a bad lot, are they?" I boasted.

Sylvia agreed with my assessment of my family.

"There is something I've not told you that happened whilst you were away."

"What?" I asked.

"I went to see the osteopath to ask his opinion of your condition."

"No matter whatever he says, I have definitely given up 'the ring'."

Before giving me Mick's considered opinion of my health, Sylvia hesitated. "He doesn't want another bout with you. In fact, he believes that you will be completely bedridden within three months."

"Not a chance. After this holiday I'll go back into strict training and next time I'll win in the first round."

"I knew that would be your attitude so I'll give you three guesses as to what I said to him when he offered to come around to massage your bedsores."

"Sylvia, my dear, you know I don't know any of the likely words."

After deciding that we would together prove how wrong the average osteopath can be, we turned out the light. I am not sure if my wife went straight off to sleep but I lay considering what the future held in store and whether the osteopath could be correct. My thoughts drifted back over many years to the time I was in my early teens. At that time, I was enjoying a very happy and active life.

My father was always the Secretary and occasionally the President of my hometown's Chamber of Trade and, because he held these positions, my sister and I attended, in company with Mum and Dad, all the main functions in the town's social calendar. To more elevated persons, the President's Evening, Police Ball and Mayor's Ball no doubt appeared small time and unsophisticated but, to us unashamed small timers, they were the highlights of the year. Invariably they would commence at half past seven in the evening and continue until as late as one o'clock in the morning. It was to these unforgettable occasions that my mother compared 'life' during a discussion I had with her in those long past years to which my thoughts had drifted.

"The way I look at life, Bob," Mother said to her 12 or 13 year old son, "is the way I look at a late-night dance. When we first arrive, we would argue with anyone who wanted us to go home. At the interval, still we would hate to go home but, by midnight, it wouldn't be all that upsetting. However, when the band has played the last waltz and the national anthem we are quite prepared, if not happy, to leave it all behind, go home to bed, and then off to a lovely sleep."

This, to the best of my memory, was the only piece of outright non-political philosophy my Mum ever gave to me but it has been my favourite and best remembered. As my thoughts slowly returned to this night prior to our first holiday as shopkeepers, I firmly decided that, perhaps, I was just a little 'life-soiled' but we had only just finished the first few dances.

Afterword
BY CATHY GORDON

So, there are some of the many stories about my family and, in particular, how my father lived with MS. I hope it comes across how Dad lived life to the full and tried his best to make sure that MS was merely an inconvenience to him whilst living life to the full.

The last words in this book about life being a party, which is in the last chapter of this book, said by my grandma, (which is something I repeat to my friends also), I have taken, remain with me and are often repeated to my friends. As such, as I head to the 'slowing down' part and, true to how Dad decided to share our world, I have decided to continue our stories. Like my father when he wrote this book, I am not quite ready to 'go to bed' yet and have enjoyed many areas of life, several with mad moments, so it would only be fair to continue this book with a few more stories from Dad and some from my own life, thankfully without 'MS'.

Thank you for reading this very special book and I very much look forward to joining you all again with my version of 'In a MeSs'. Why don't you follow me on my journey by joining https://www.facebook.com/bobinamess and share your own MS stories.

Lightning Source UK Ltd.
Milton Keynes UK
UKOW04f0222250914

239125UK00001B/18/P

9 781783 014644